A NATIONAL SECURITY STRATEGY OF ENGAGEMENT AND ENLARGEMENT 1995–1996

Also available from Brassey's:

NATIONAL SECURITY STRATEGY OF THE
UNITED STATES
by Ronald Reagan (1988)

NATIONAL SECURITY STRATEGY OF THE
UNITED STATES: 1990–1991
by George Bush (1990)

NATIONAL SECURITY STRATEGY OF THE
UNITED STATES: 1994–1995
by William J. Clinton (1994)

A NATIONAL SECURITY STRATEGY
OF ENGAGEMENT AND ENLARGEMENT
1995–1996

WILLIAM J. CLINTON

BRASSEY'S
Washington • London

First Brassey's edition 1995
This work was originally released as a public document by the
White House in February 1995 under the title *A National Security
Strategy of Engagement and Enlargement*.
ISBN 1-57488-021-9

10 9 8 7 6 5 4 3 2 1
Printed in the United States of America

Publisher's Note

A National Security Strategy of Engagement and Enlargement is the President's articulation to the U.S. Congress of American strategic objectives. Brassey's is pleased to publish this public document to ensure that it is broadly available to American citizens, who remain vitally interested in our nation's role in the world.

Franklin D. Margiotta, Ph.D.

President and Publisher
Brassey's, Inc.

 **An AUSA Book**

The Association of the United States Army, or AUSA, was founded in 1950 as a not-for-profit organization dedicated to education concerning the role of the U.S. Army, to providing material for military professional development, and to the promotion of proper recognition and appreciation of the profession of arms. Its constituencies include those who serve in the Army today, including Army National Guard, Army Reserve, and Army civilians, and the retirees and veterans who have served in the past, and all their families. A large number of public-minded citizens and business leaders are also an important constituency. The Association seeks to educate the public, elected and appointed officials, and leaders of the defense industry on crucial issues involving the adequacy of our national defense, particularly those issues affecting land warfare.

In 1988 AUSA established within its existing organization a new entity known as the Institute of

Land Warfare. Its purpose is to extend the educational work of AUSA by sponsoring scholarly publications, to include books, monographs, and essays on key defense issues, as well as workshops and symposia. Among the volumes chosen for designation as "An AUSA Institute of Land Warfare Book" are both new texts and reprints of titles of enduring value that are no longer in print. Topics include history, policy issues, strategy, and tactics. Publication as an AUSA book does not indicate that the Association of the United States Army and the publisher agree with everything in the book, but does suggest that the AUSA and the publisher believe it will stimulate the thinking of AUSA members and others concerned about important issues.

Contents

Preface — xi

I. Introduction — 1

II. Advancing Our Interests Through Engagement and Enlargement — 25

ENHANCING OUR SECURITY — 31

MAINTAINING A STRONG DEFENSE CAPABILITY — 33

- Major Regional Contingencies — 37
- Overseas Presence — 39
- Counterterrorism, Fighting Drug Trafficking and Other Missions — 41
  - *Combating Terrorism* — 42
  - *Fighting Drug Trafficking* — 44
  - *Other Missions* — 46

DECIDING WHEN AND HOW TO EMPLOY U.S. FORCES — 49

COMBATING THE SPREAD AND USE OF WEAPONS OF MASS DESTRUCTION AND MISSILES — 56

- Nonproliferation and Counterproliferation — 56
- Nuclear Forces — 62

ARMS CONTROL — 63

PEACE OPERATIONS — 68

STRONG INTELLIGENCE CAPABILITIES — 73

THE ENVIRONMENT AND SUSTAINABLE DEVELOPMENT — 78

PROMOTING PROSPERITY AT HOME	80
ENHANCING AMERICAN COMPETITIVENESS	81
PARTNERSHIP WITH BUSINESS AND LABOR	82
ENHANCING ACCESS TO FOREIGN MARKETS	84
The North American Free Trade Agreement	84
Asia-Pacific Economic Cooperation	85
Uruguay Round of GATT	86
U.S.-Japan Framework Agreement	87
Summit of the Americas	88
Expanding the Realm of Free Trade	88
STRENGTHENING MACROECONOMIC COORDINATION	89
PROVIDING FOR ENERGY SECURITY	90
PROMOTING SUSTAINABLE DEVELOPMENT ABROAD	91
PROMOTING DEMOCRACY	96
III. Integrated Regional Approaches	**107**
EUROPE AND EURASIA	109
EAST ASIA AND THE PACIFIC	122
THE WESTERN HEMISPHERE	129
THE MIDDLE EAST, SOUTHWEST AND SOUTH ASIA	132
AFRICA	136
IV. Conclusions	**141**

Preface

Protecting our nation's security—our people, our territory and our way of life—is my Administration's foremost mission and constitutional duty. The end of the Cold War fundamentally changed America's security imperatives. The central security challenge of the past half century—the threat of communist expansion—is gone. The dangers we face today are more diverse. Ethnic conflict is spreading and rogue states pose a serious danger to regional stability in many corners of the globe. The proliferation of weapons of mass destruction represents a major challenge to our security. Large-scale environmental degradation, exacerbated by rapid population growth, threatens to undermine political stability in many countries and regions.

At the same time, we have unparalleled opportunities to make our nation safer and more prosperous. Our military might is unparalleled. We now have a truly global economy linked by an instantaneous communications network, which offers growing opportunity for American jobs and American investment. The community of democratic nations is growing, enhancing the prospects for political stability, peaceful conflict resolution and greater dignity and hope for the people of the world. The international community is beginning to act together to address pressing global environmental needs.

Never has American leadership been more essential—to navigate the shoals of the world's new dangers and to capitalize on its opportunities. American assets are unique: our military strength, our dynamic economy, our powerful ideals and, above all, our people. We can and must make the difference through our engagement; but our involvement must be carefully tailored to serve our interests and priorities.

This report, submitted in accordance with Section 603 of the Goldwater-Nichols Defense Department Reorganization Act of 1986, elaborates a national security strategy tailored for this new era. Focusing on new threats and new opportunities, its central goals are:

Engagement and Enlargement: 1995-1996

- To sustain our security with military forces that are ready to fight.
- To bolster America's economic revitalization.
- To promote democracy abroad.

Over the past two years, my Administration has worked diligently to pursue these goals. This national security strategy report presents the strategy that has guided this effort. It is premised on a belief that the line between our domestic and foreign policies is disappearing—that we must revitalize our economy if we are to sustain our military forces, foreign initiatives and global influence, and that we must engage actively abroad if we are to open foreign markets and create jobs for our people.

We believe that our goals of enhancing our security, bolstering our economic prosperity, and promoting democracy are mutually supportive. Secure nations are more likely to support free trade and maintain democratic structures. Nations with growing economies and strong trade ties are more likely to feel secure and to work toward freedom. And democratic states are less likely to threaten our interests and more likely to cooperate with the U.S. to meet security threats and promote free trade and sustainable development.

Since my Administration began, we have been deeply engaged in adapting existing structures, and in constructing new ones, to meet these goals. To enhance global security, for example, we have pursued peace initiatives in the Middle East; established NATO's Partnership for Peace and initiated a process that will lead to NATO's expansion; secured the accession of Ukraine, Kazakhstan, and Belarus to the Nuclear Non-Proliferation Treaty and their agreement to eliminate nuclear weapons from their territory, which in turn opened the door to the ratification and entry into force of the START I Treaty; participated in an unprecedented regional security gathering of the ASEAN countries and others, including Russia and Vietnam; and reached an agreed framework with North Korea that halted, and will eventually eliminate, its dangerous nuclear program. To bolster prosperity at home and around the world, we have secured the enactment of legislation implementing both the North American Free Trade Agreement (NAFTA) and the Uruguay Round of the General Agreement on Tariffs and Trade (GATT), worked to open Asian-Pacific markets through two leaders meetings of the Asia-Pacific Economic Cooperation forum, lowered export controls and held a Western Hemisphere Summit in Miami where the 34 democratic nations of this hemisphere committed themselves to negotiate a free trade agreement by 2005. To promote democracy, we have supported South Africa's recent transformation, provided aid to a new democratic Russia and other new independent states as well as Central and Eastern European nations, assisted Cambodia, and worked with our Western Hemisphere neighbors restoring the democratically elected government in Haiti and hosting the Summit of the Americas, which reaffirmed and strengthened our mutual commitment to democracy.

Our extraordinary diplomatic leverage to reshape existing security and economic structures and create new ones ultimately relies upon

American power. Our economic and military might, as well as the power of our ideals, make America's diplomats the first among equals. Our economic strength gives us a position of advantage on almost every global issue. For instance, South Africa and our negotiations with North Korea demonstrate how economic incentives and the imposition—or the threat—of economic sanctions enable us to achieve our objectives as part of our determined diplomacy.

But military force remains an indispensable element of our nation's power. Even with the Cold War over, our nation must maintain military forces sufficient to deter diverse threats and, when necessary, to fight and win against our adversaries. While many factors ultimately contribute to our nation's safety and well-being, no single component is more important than the men and women who wear America's uniform and stand sentry over our security. Their skill, service and dedication constitute the core of our defenses. Today our military is the best-equipped, best-trained and best-prepared fighting force in the world. Time after time in the last year, our troops demonstrated their current readiness and strength: helping to save hundreds of thousands of lives in Rwanda; moving with lightning speed to head off another Iraqi threat to Kuwait; and giving freedom and democracy back to the people of Haiti. I am committed to ensuring that this military capability is not compromised.

The United States recognizes that we have a special responsibility that goes along with being a great power. Our global interests and our historic ideals impel us to oppose those who would endanger the survival or well-being of their peaceful neighbors. Nations should be able to expect that their borders and their sovereignty will always be secure. At the same time, this does not mean we or the international community must tolerate gross violations of human rights within those borders.

When our national security interests are threatened, we will, as America always has, use diplomacy when we can, but force if we must. We will act with others when we can, but alone when we must. We recognize, however, that while force can defeat an aggressor, it cannot solve underlying problems. Democracy and economic prosperity can take root in a struggling society only through local solutions carried out by the society itself. We must use military force selectively, recognizing that its use may do no more than provide a window of opportunity for a society—and diplomacy—to work.

We therefore will send American troops abroad only when our interests and our values are sufficiently at stake. When we do so, it will be with clear objectives to which we are firmly committed and which—when combat is likely—we have the means to achieve decisively. To do otherwise, risks those objectives and endangers our troops. These requirements are as pertinent for humanitarian and other non-traditional interventions today as they were for previous generations during prolonged world wars. Modern media communications may now bring to our homes both the suffering that exists in many parts of the world and the casualties that may accompany interventions to help. But we must remain clear in our purpose and resolute in its execution. And while we must continue to reassess the costs and benefits of any operation as it unfolds, reflexive calls for with-

Engagement and Enlargement: 1995-1996

drawal of our forces when casualties are incurred would simply encourage rogue actors to try to force our departure from areas where there are U.S. interests by attacking American troops.

During the past two years, diplomacy backed by American power has produced results:

- When Iraq moved forces toward Kuwait, we reacted swiftly and dispatched large-scale forces to the region under the authority of the United Nations—but were prepared to act alone, if necessary.

- In Haiti, it was only when the Haitian military learned that the 82nd Airborne Division was enroute that we achieved peacefully what we were prepared to do under fire.

- In Bosnia, we have been able to achieve limited but important objectives when diplomacy has been married to appropriate military power. For instance, the Sarajevo ultimatum largely succeeded because the threat of NATO air power was judged real; similarly, the threat of NATO airpower prevented the fall of Gorazde.

- In Rwanda and Somalia, only the American military could have done what it did in these humanitarian missions, saving hundreds of thousands of lives. However, over the longer run our interests were served by turning these operations over to multilateral peacekeeping forces once the immediate humanitarian crisis was addressed. No outside force can create a stable and legitimate domestic order for another society—that work can only be accomplished by the society itself.

Our national security strategy reflects both America's interests and our values. Our commitment to freedom, equality and human dignity continues to serve as a beacon of hope to peoples around the world. The vitality, creativity and diversity of American society are important sources of national strength in a global economy increasingly driven by information and ideas.

Engagement and Enlargement: 1995-1996

Our prospects in this new era are promising. The specter of nuclear annihilation has dramatically receded. The historic events of the past two years—including the handshake between Israel and the PLO, the peace treaty between Israel and Jordan, and the transformation of South Africa to a multiracial democracy headed by President Mandela—suggest this era's possibilities for achieving security, prosperity and democracy.

Our nation can only address this era's dangers and opportunities if we remain actively engaged in global affairs. We are the world's greatest power, and we have global interests as well as responsibilities. As our nation learned after World War I, we can find no security for America in isolationism nor prosperity in protectionism. For the American people to be safer and enjoy expanding opportunities, our nation must work to deter would-be aggressors, open foreign markets, promote the spread of democracy abroad, encourage sustainable development and pursue new opportunities for peace.

Our national security requires the patient application of American will and resources. We can only sustain that necessary investment with the broad, bipartisan support of the American people and their representatives in Congress. The full participation of Congress is essential to the success of our new engagement, and I will consult with members of Congress at every step in making and implementing American foreign policy. The Cold War may be over, but the need for American leadership abroad remains as strong as ever. I am committed to forging a new public consensus to sustain our active engagement abroad in pursuit of our cherished goal—a more secure world where democracy and free markets know no borders. This document details that commitment.

·I· INTRODUCTION

A new era is upon us. The Cold War is over. The dissolution of the Soviet empire has radically transformed the security environment facing the United States and our allies. The primary security imperative of the past half century—containing communist expansion while preventing nuclear war—is gone. We no longer face massive Soviet forces across an East-West divide nor Soviet missiles targeted on the United States. Yet there remains a complex array of new and old security challenges America must meet as we approach a new century.

This national security strategy assesses America's role in this new international context and describes the Administration's strategy to advance our interests at home and abroad.

This is a period of great promise but also great uncertainty. We stand as the world's preeminent power. America's core value of freedom, as embodied in democratic governance and market economics, has gained ground around the world. Hundreds of millions of people have thrown off communism, dictatorship or apartheid. Former adversaries now cooperate with us in diplomacy and global problem solving. Both the threat of a war among great powers and the specter of nuclear annihilation have receded dramatically. The dynamism of the global economy is transforming commerce, culture and global politics, promising greater prosperity for America and greater cooperation among nations.

At the same time, troubling uncertainties and clear threats remain. The new, independent states that replaced the Soviet Union are experiencing wrenching economic and political transitions, as are many new democracies of Central and Eastern Europe. While our relations with the other great powers are as constructive as at any point in this century, Russia's historic transformation will proceed along a difficult path, and China maintains a repressive regime even as that country assumes a more important economic and political role in global affairs. The spread of weapons of mass destruction poses serious threats. Violent extremists threaten fragile peace processes in many parts of the world. Worldwide, there is a resurgence of militant nationalism as well as ethnic and religious conflict. This has been demonstrated by upheavals in Bosnia, Rwanda and Somalia, where the United States has participated in peacekeeping and humanitarian missions.

Not all security risks are immediate or military in nature. Transnational phenomena such as terrorism, narcotics trafficking, environmental degradation, natural resource depletion, rapid population growth and refugee flows also have security implications for both present and long-term American policy. In addition, an emerging class of transnational environmental issues are increasingly affecting international stability and consequently will present new challenges to U.S. strategy.

American leadership in the world has never been more important, for there is a simple truth about this new world: the same idea that was under attack three times in this century—first by imperialism and then by fascism and communism—remains under attack today, but on many fronts at once. It is an idea that comes under many names—democracy, liberty, civility, pluralism—but which together are the values of a society where leaders and governments preserve individual freedoms, and ensure opportunity and human dignity. As the President has said, "We face a contest as old as history—a struggle between freedom and tyranny; between tolerance and isolation. It is a fight between those who would build free societies governed by laws and those who would impose their will by force. Our struggle today, in a world more high-tech, more fast-moving, more chaotically diverse than ever, is the age-old fight between hope and fear."

The victors of World War I squandered their triumph in this age-old struggle when they turned inward, bringing on a global depression and allowing fascism to rise, and reigniting global war. After World War II, we learned the lessons of the past. In the face of a new totalitarian threat this great nation did not walk away from the challenge of the moment. Instead it chose to reach out, to rebuild international security structures and to lead. This determination of previous generations to prevail over communism by shaping new international structures left us a world stronger, safer and freer. It is this example and its success which now inspire us to begin the difficult task of a new stage in this old struggle: to secure the peace won in the Cold War against those who would still deny people their human rights, terrorists who threaten innocents and pariah states who choose repression and extremism over openness and moderation.

If we exert our leadership abroad, we can make America safer and more prosperous—by deterring aggression, by fostering the peaceful resolution of dangerous conflicts, by opening foreign markets, by helping democratic regimes and by tackling global problems. Without our active leadership and engagement abroad, threats will fester and our opportunities will narrow.

We must seek to be as creative and constructive—in the literal sense of that word—as the generation of the late 1940's. For all its dangers, this new world presents an immense opportunity—the chance to adapt and construct global institutions that will help to provide security and increase economic growth throughout the world.

The issue for the next decade is whether our efforts at this construction can succeed in the face of shifting threats to the ideals and habits of democracy. It is therefore in our interest that democracy be at once the foundation and the purpose of the international structures we build through this constructive diplomacy: the foundation, because the institutions will be a reflection of their shared values and norms; the purpose, because if our economic institutions are secure, democracy will flourish.

While democracy will not soon take hold everywhere, we know that the larger the pool of democracies, the better off we, and the entire community of nations, will be. Democracies create free markets that offer economic opportunity, make for more reliable trading partners, and are far less likely to wage war on one another. It is in our interest to do all that we can to enlarge the community of free and open societies, especially in areas of greatest strategic interest, as in the former Soviet Union.

We can only engage actively abroad if the American people and the Congress are willing to bear the costs of that leadership—in dollars, political energy and, at times, American lives. In a democracy, the foreign policy of the nation must serve the needs of the people. The preamble of the Constitution sets out the basic objectives:

> *to provide for the common defense, promote the general welfare, and secure the blessings of liberty to ourselves and our posterity.*

The end of the Cold War does not alter these fundamental purposes. Nor does it reduce the need for active American efforts, here and abroad, to pursue those goals. One purpose of this report is to help foster the broad, bipartisan understanding and support necessary to sustain our international engagement. A coalition of the center through bipartisan congressional participation is critical to this commitment.

Our national security strategy is based on enlarging the community of market democracies while deterring and containing a range of threats to our nation, our allies and our interests. The more that democracy and political and economic liberalization take hold in the world, particularly in countries of geostrategic importance to us, the safer our nation is likely to be and the more our people are likely to prosper.

To that broad end, the report explains the three central components of our strategy of engagement and enlargement: our efforts to enhance our security by maintaining a strong defense capability and promoting cooperative security measures; our work to open foreign markets and spur global economic growth; and our promotion of democracy abroad. It also explains how we are pursuing the three elements of our strategy in specific regions by adapting and constructing institutions that will help to provide security and increase economic growth throughout the world.

During the first two years of this Administration, this strategy already has produced tangible results with respect to our security requirements:

- At the President's direction, the Pentagon completed the Bottom Up Review, a full-scale assessment of what defense forces and systems our nation needs for this new security era. The President has also set forth a defense budget for Fiscal Years 1996–2001 that funds the force structure recommended by the Review, and he repeatedly stressed that he will draw the line against further cuts that would undermine that force structure or erode U.S. military readiness. The swift and efficient deployment of our forces last October to the Persian Gulf, and to Haiti and Rwanda, clearly demonstrates their continued readiness to respond as needed. The President also requested Congress to enact supplemental appropriations of $1.7 billion for FY 1994 and $2.6 billion for FY 1995 to ensure training readiness is not impaired by the costs of such unanticipated contingencies. In addition, the President added $25 billion to the defense spending plan over the next six years to provide more funding for readiness and to improve the quality of life of our military personnel and families.

- At President Clinton's initiative, a NATO Summit in January 1994 approved the

Partnership For Peace (PFP) and initiated a process that will lead to NATO's gradual expansion to ensure that NATO is prepared to meet the European and trans-Atlantic security challenges of this era, and to provide the security relationships that will provide the underpinnings for the democratic gains in Europe since 1989. Since the Summit, 25 countries, including Russia, agreed to join the Partnership for Peace.

- The United States, Russia, Ukraine, Belarus and Kazakhstan exchanged instruments of ratification for the START I Treaty at the December summit of the Conference on Security and Cooperation in Europe (CSCE), culminating two years of intensive U.S. diplomatic efforts to bring the Treaty into force and paving the way for ratification of the START II Treaty. START I requires the permanent elimination of bombers, ICBM silos and ballistic missile submarine launch tubes that carried over 9,000 of the 21,000 total warheads the United States and the former Soviet Union declared when the Treaty was signed—a reduction of 40 percent. START II, signed in 1993, will eliminate additional U.S. and Russian strategic launchers and will effectively remove an additional 5,000 warheads, leaving each side with no more than 3,500. These actions will reduce the strategic force arsenals of the United States and Russia by two-thirds. Presidents Clinton and Yeltsin have agreed that once START II is ratified, the United States and Russia will begin immediately to deactivate all strategic nuclear delivery systems to be reduced under the Treaty by removing their nuclear warheads or taking other steps to take them out of combat status, thus removing thousands of warheads from alert status years ahead of schedule. The two Presidents also directed an intensification of dialogue regarding the possibility of further reductions of, and limitations on, remaining nuclear forces.

- The President launched a comprehensive policy to combat the proliferation of weapons of mass destruction and the missiles that deliver them. The United States has secured landmark commitments to eliminate all nuclear weapons from Ukraine, Belarus and Kazakhstan and, in December, all three nations formally acceded to the Nuclear Nonproliferation Treaty as non-nuclear weapon states. The United States and over 30 other nations opened formal negotiations on a Comprehensive Test Ban Treaty in January 1994, producing a Joint Draft Treaty text that provides a baseline for resolving remaining issues. We also made significant progress during the past year in negotiations within the Anti-Ballistic Missile (ABM) Treaty's Standing Consultative Commission (SCC) to establish an agreed demarcation between strategic and theater ballistic missiles that will allow for the deployment of advanced theater missile defense and update the ABM treaty to reflect the break-up of the Soviet Union. The Administration also submitted the Chemical Weapons Convention to the

Senate for ratification and supported the development of new measures to strengthen the Biological Weapons Convention.

- The Administration reached an important agreed framework with North Korea that has halted, and will eventually eliminate, that country's nuclear program, greatly enhancing regional stability and achieving our nonproliferation goals. The Administration also reached agreements with Russia, Ukraine and South Africa to control missile-related technology and secured China's commitment not to transfer MTCR-controlled ground-to-ground missiles.

- The President's efforts helped bring about many historic firsts in the Middle East peace process—the handshake of peace between Prime Minister Rabin and Chairman Arafat on the White House lawn has been followed by the Jordan-Israel peace treaty, progress on eliminating the Arab boycott of Israel and the establishment of ties between Israel and an increasing number of its Arab neighbors.

- On May 3, 1994, President Clinton signed a Presidential Decision Directive establishing "U.S. Policy on Reforming Multilateral Peace Operations." This policy represents the first, comprehensive framework for U.S. decisionmaking on issues of peacekeeping and peace enforcement suited to the realities of the post–Cold War period.

- In October 1994, President Clinton submitted the United Nations Convention on the Law of the Sea to the Senate for ratification. This was the culmination of years of negotiations to ensure an equitable balance between the rights of coastal states to control activities in adjacent offshore areas to protect their economic, security and environmental interests, and the rights of maritime states to free and unimpeded navigation and overflight of the oceans of the world. This included an acceptable regime to administer the mineral resources of the deep seabed, thereby protecting U.S. interests.

On the economic front, Administration policies have created nearly six million American jobs and established the foundation for the global economy of the 21st century:

- The President worked with the Congress on effective measures to reduce the federal budget deficit and restore economic growth. These measures help increase our competitiveness and strengthen our position in negotiations with other nations.

- The President secured approval of the North American Free Trade Agreement (NAFTA) which creates the world's largest free trade zone and has already created more than 100,000 American jobs. The vote for NAFTA marked a decisive U.S. affirmation of its international engagement. Through NAFTA's environmental and labor side agreements, we are working actively to protect the rights of workers and to reduce air and water pollution that crosses national boundaries. When Mexico came under short-term financial pressures in December of 1994, the United States took the lead in marshaling international support to assist the country in meeting this challenge. This decision reflected the President's belief that the United States has a strong interest in prosperity and stability in Mexico and that it is in our economic and strategic interest that Mexico's economic reform program succeeds.

- The Administration stood at the forefront of a multilateral effort to achieve history's most extensive market-opening agreements in the GATT Uruguay-round negotiations on world trade. Working with a bipartisan coalition in the Congress, the President secured approval of this pathbreaking agreement and the resulting World Trade Organization, which will add $100–200 billion and hundreds of thousands of jobs each year to the U.S. economy.

- The President convened the first meeting of leaders of the Asia-Pacific Economic Cooperation (APEC) forum—and took steps to expand our ties with the economies of the Asia-Pacific region, the fastest growing area in the world. At their second meeting in November 1994, the APEC leaders agreed to the goal of free trade within the region by early in the 21st century and to develop a blueprint for implementation by the APEC meeting this year in Osaka.

- The President hosted the Summit of the Americas in December, a historic gathering where the 34 democratic nations of the hemisphere committed themselves to completing negotiations on a regional free trade agreement by 2005. In Miami, the United States, Canada and Mexico also invited Chile to begin negotiations to join NAFTA.

- We have committed the United States to reduce its greenhouse gas emissions to 1990 levels by the year 2000, and we have developed a National Climate Plan to achieve that goal. The United States has also taken a leading role at the international level toward phasing out the production of most ozone-depleting substances. Under the Montreal Protocol for the protection of the ozone layer, the United States is contributing to developing countries' efforts to reduce their emissions of ozone-depleting chemicals. In June 1993, the U.S. signed the Biodiversity Treaty, and one year later, the Desertification Convention.

- The Administration has asserted world leadership on population issues. We played a key role during the Cairo Conference on Population and Development in developing a consensus Program of Action, including increased availability of voluntary family planning and reproductive health services, sustainable economic development, strengthening of family ties, the empowerment of women including enhanced educational opportunities, and a reduction in infant and child mortality through immunizations and other programs.

Engagement and Enlargement: 1995–1996

Finally, the President has demonstrated a firm commitment to expanding the global realm of democracy:

- The Administration substantially expanded U.S. support for democratic and market reform in Russia, Ukraine and the other newly independent states of the former Soviet Union, including a comprehensive assistance package for Ukraine.

- The United States launched a series of initiatives to bolster the new democracies of Central and Eastern Europe, including the White House Trade and Investment Conference for Central and Eastern Europe held in Cleveland in January. We affirmed our concern for their security and market economic transformation, recognizing that such assurances would play a key role in promoting democratic developments.

- Working with the international community under the auspices of the UN, we succeeded in reversing the coup in Haiti and restoring the democratically elected president and government. We are now helping the Haitian people consolidate their hard-won democracy and rebuild their country as we complete the transition from the Multinational Force to the United Nations Mission in Haiti.

- U.S. engagement in Northern Ireland contributed to the establishment of a cease-fire, first by the IRA and subsequently by loyalist para-militaries. The President announced in November a package of initiatives aimed at consolidating the peace by promoting economic revitalization and increased private sector trade and investment in Northern Ireland.

- At the Summit of the Americas, the 34 democratic nations of the hemisphere agreed to a detailed plan of cooperative action in such diverse fields as health, education, counternarcotics, environmental protection, information infrastructure, and the strengthening and safeguarding of democratic institutions, in addition to mutual prosperity and sustainable development. The Summit ushered in a new era of hemispheric cooperation that would not have been possible without U.S. leadership and commitment.

- The United States has increased support for South Africa as it conducted elections and became a multiracial democracy. During the state visit of Nelson Mandela in October, we announced formation of a bilateral commission to foster new cooperation between our nations, and an assistance package to support housing, health, education, trade and investment.

- The United States, working with the Organization of American States, helped reverse an anti-democratic coup in Guatemala.

- In Mozambique and Angola, the United States played a leading role in galvanizing the international community to help bring an end to two decades of civil war and to promote national reconciliation. For the first time, there is the prospect that all of southern Africa will enjoy the fruits of peace and prosperity.

- The Administration initiated policies aimed at crisis prevention, including a new peacekeeping policy.

This report has two major sections. The first part of the report explains our strategy of engagement and enlargement. The second part describes briefly how the Administration is applying this strategy to the world's major regions.

·II·
ADVANCING OUR INTERESTS THROUGH ENGAGEMENT AND ENLARGEMENT

The dawn of the post–Cold War era presents the United States with many distinct dangers, but also with a generally improved security environment and a range of opportunities to improve it further. The unitary threat that dominated our engagement during the Cold War has been replaced by a complex set of challenges. Our nation's strategy for defining and addressing those challenges has several core principles which guide our policy. First and foremost, we must exercise global leadership. We are not the world's policeman, but as the world's premier economic and military power, and with the strength of our democratic values, the U.S. is indispensable to the forging of stable political relations and open trade.

Our leadership must stress preventive diplomacy—through such means as support for democracy, economic assistance, overseas military presence, military-to-military contacts and involvement in multilateral negotiations in the Middle East and elsewhere—in order to help resolve problems, reduce tensions and defuse conflicts before they become crises. These measures are a wise investment in our national security because they offer the prospect of resolving problems with the least human and material cost.

Our engagement must be selective, focusing on the challenges that are most relevant to our own interests and focusing our resources where we can make the most difference. We must also use the right tools—being willing to act unilaterally when our direct national interests are most at stake; in alliance and partnership when our interests are shared by others; and multilaterally when our interests are more general and the problems are best addressed by the international community. In all cases, the nature of our response must depend on what best serves our own long-term national interests. Those interests are ultimately defined by our security requirements. Such requirements start with our physical defense and economic well-being. They also include environmental security as well as the security of values achieved through expansion of the community of democratic nations.

Our national security strategy draws upon a range of political, military and economic instruments, and focuses on the primary objectives that President Clinton has stressed throughout his Administration:

- Enhancing Our Security. Taking account of the realities of the post–Cold War era and the new threats, a military capability appropriately sized and postured to meet the diverse needs of our strategy, including the ability, in concert with regional allies, to win two nearly simultaneous major regional conflicts. We will continue to pursue arms control agreements to reduce the danger of nuclear, chemical, biological, and conventional conflict and to promote stability.

- Promoting Prosperity at Home. A vigorous and integrated economic policy designed to stimulate global environmentally sound economic growth and free trade and to press for open and equal U.S. access to foreign markets.

- Promoting Democracy. A framework of

democratic enlargement that increases our security by protecting, consolidating and enlarging the community of free market democracies. Our efforts focus on strengthening democratic processes in key emerging democratic states including Russia, Ukraine and other new states of the former Soviet Union.

These basic objectives of our national security strategy will guide the allocation of our scarce national security resources. Because deficit reduction is also central to the long-term health and competitiveness of the American economy, we have made it, along with efficient and environmentally sound use of our resources, a major priority. Under the Clinton economic plan, the deficit will be reduced over 700 billion dollars by Fiscal Year 1998. President Clinton has also lowered the deficit as a percentage of the Gross Domestic Product from 4.9 percent in Fiscal Year 1992 to 2.4 percent in Fiscal Year 1995—the lowest since 1979.

Enhancing Our Security

The U.S. government is responsible for protecting the lives and personal safety of Americans, maintaining our political freedom and independence as a nation and promoting the well-being and prosperity of our nation. No matter how powerful we are as a nation, we cannot secure these basic goals unilaterally. Whether the problem is nuclear proliferation, regional instability, the reversal of reform in the former Soviet empire or unfair trade practices, the threats and challenges we face demand cooperative, multinational solutions. Therefore, the only responsible U.S. strategy is one that seeks to ensure U.S. influence over and participation in collective decisionmaking in a wide and growing range of circumstances.

An important element of our security preparedness depends on durable relationships with allies and other friendly nations. Accordingly, a central thrust of our strategy of engagement is to sustain and adapt the security relationships we have with key nations around the world. These ties constitute an important part of an international framework that will be essential to ensuring cooperation across a broad range of issues. Within the realm of security issues, our cooperation with allies includes such activities as: conducting combined training and exercises, coordinating military plans and preparations, sharing intelligence, jointly developing new systems and controlling exports of sensitive technologies according to common standards.

The post–Cold War era presents a different set of threats to our security. In this new period, enhancing American security requires, first and foremost, developing and maintaining a strong defense capability of forces ready to fight.

We are developing integrated approaches for dealing with threats arising from the development of nuclear and other weapons of mass destruction by other nations. Our security requires a vigorous arms control effort and a strong intelligence capability. We have implemented a strategy for multilateral peace operations. We have clarified rigorous guidelines for when and how to use military force in this era.

We also face security risks that are not solely military in nature. Transnational phenomena such as terrorism, narcotics trafficking, and refugee flows also have security implications both for present and long-term American policy. An emerging class of transnational environmental and natural resource issues is increasingly affecting international stability and consequently will present new challenges to U.S. strategy. The threat of intrusions to our military and commercial information systems poses a significant risk to national security and must be addressed.

Maintaining a Strong Defense Capability

U.S. military capabilities are critical to the success of our strategy. This nation has unparalleled military capabilities: the United States is the only nation capable of conducting large-scale and effective military operations far beyond its borders. This fact, coupled with our unique position as the security partner of choice in many regions, provides a foundation for regional stability through mutually beneficial security partnerships. Our willingness and ability to play a leading role in defending common interests also help ensure that the United States will remain an influential voice in international affairs—political, military and economic—that affect our well-being, so long as we retain the military wherewithal to underwrite our commitments credibly.

To protect and advance U.S. interests in the face of the dangers and opportunities outlined earlier, the United States must deploy robust and flexible military forces that can accomplish a variety of tasks:

- Deterring and Defeating Aggression in Major Regional Conflicts. Our forces must be able to help offset the military power of regional states with interests opposed to those of the United States and its allies. To do this, we must be able to credibly deter and defeat aggression, by projecting and sustaining U.S. power in more than one region if necessary.

- Providing a Credible Overseas Presence. U.S. forces must also be forward deployed or stationed in key overseas regions in peacetime to deter aggression and advance U.S. strategic interests. Such overseas presence demonstrates our commitment to allies and friends, underwrites regional stability, gains us familiarity with overseas operating environments, promotes combined training among the forces of friendly countries and provides timely initial response capabilities.

- Countering Weapons of Mass Destruction. We are devoting greater efforts to stemming the proliferation of weapons of mass destruction and their delivery means, but at the same time we must improve our capabilities to deter and prevent the use of such weapons and protect ourselves against their effects.

- Contributing to Multilateral Peace Operations. When our interests call for it, the United States must also be prepared to participate in multilateral efforts to resolve regional conflicts and bolster new democratic governments. Thus, our forces must be ready to participate in peacekeeping, peace enforcement and other operations in support of these objectives.

- **Supporting Counterterrorism Efforts and Other National Security Objectives.** A number of other tasks remain that U.S. forces have typically carried out with both general purpose and specialized units. These missions include: counterterrorism and punitive attacks, noncombatant evacuation, counternarcotics operations, special forces assistance to nations and humanitarian and disaster relief operations.

To meet all of these requirements successfully, our forces must be capable of responding quickly and operating effectively. That is, they must be ready to fight and win. This imperative demands highly qualified and motivated people; modern, well-maintained equipment; realistic training; strategic mobility; sufficient support and sustainment capabilities, and proper investment in science and technology.

Major Regional Contingencies

The focus of our planning for major theater conflict is on deterring and, if necessary, fighting and defeating aggression by potentially hostile regional powers, such as North Korea, Iran or Iraq. Such states are capable of fielding sizable military forces that can cause serious imbalances in military power within regions important to the United States, with allied or friendly states often finding it difficult to match the power of a potentially aggressive neighbor. To deter aggression, prevent coercion of allied or friendly governments and, ultimately, defeat aggression should it occur, we must prepare our forces to confront this scale of threat, preferably in concert with our allies and friends, but unilaterally if necessary. To do this, we must have forces that can deploy quickly and supplement U.S. forward-based and forward-deployed forces, along with regional allies, in halting an invasion and defeating the aggressor, just as we demonstrated by our rapid response in October 1994 when Iraq threatened aggression against Kuwait.

With programmed enhancements, the forces the Administration is fielding will be sufficient to help defeat aggression in two nearly simultaneous major regional conflicts. As a nation with global interests, it is important that the United States maintain forces with aggregate capabilities on this scale. Obviously, we seek to avoid a situation in which an aggressor in one region might be tempted to take advantage when U.S. forces are heavily committed elsewhere. More basically, maintaining a "two war" force helps ensure that the United States will have sufficient military capabilities to deter or defeat aggression by a coalition of hostile powers or by a larger, more capable adversary than we foresee today.

We will never know with certainty how an enemy might fight or precisely what demands might be placed on our own forces in the future. The contributions of allies or coalition partners will vary from place to place and over time. Thus, balanced U.S. forces are needed in order to provide a wide range of complementary capabilities and to cope with the unpredictable and unexpected.

Overseas Presence

The need to deploy U.S. military forces abroad in peacetime is also an important factor in determining our overall force structure. We will maintain robust overseas presence in several forms, such as permanently stationed forces and pre-positioned equipment, deployments and combined exercises, port calls and other force visits, as well as military-to-military contacts. These activities provide several benefits. Specifically they:

- Give form and substance to our bilateral and multilateral security commitments.

- Demonstrate our determination to defend U.S. and allied interests in critical regions, deterring hostile nations from acting contrary to those interests.

- Provide forward elements for rapid response in crises as well as the bases, ports and other infrastructure essential for deployment of

U.S.-based forces by air, sea and land.

- Enhance the effectiveness of coalition operations, including peace operations, by improving our ability to operate with other nations.

- Allow the United States to use its position of trust to prevent the development of power vacuums and dangerous arms races, thereby underwriting regional stability by precluding threats to regional security.

- Facilitate regional integration, since nations that may not be willing to work together in our absence may be willing to coalesce around us in a crisis.

- Promote an international security environment of trust, cooperation, peace and stability, which is fundamental to the vitality of developing democracies and free market economies for America's own economic well-being and security.

Through training programs, combined exercises, military contacts, interoperability and shared defense with potential coalition partners, as well as security assistance programs that include judicious foreign military sales, we can strengthen the local self-defense capabilities of our friends and allies. Through active participation in regional security dialogues, we can reduce regional tensions, increase transparency in armaments and improve our bilateral and multilateral cooperation.

By improving the defense capabilities of our friends and demonstrating our commitment to defend common interests, these activities enhance deterrence, encourage responsibility-sharing on the part of friends and allies, decrease the likelihood that U.S. forces will be necessary if conflict arises and raise the odds that U.S. forces will find a relatively favorable situation should a U.S. response be required.

Counterterrorism, Fighting Drug Trafficking and Other Missions

While the missions outlined above will remain the primary determinants of our general purpose and nuclear force structure, U.S. military forces and assets will also be called upon to perform a wide range of other important missions as well. Some of these can be accomplished by conventional forces fielded primarily for theater operations. Often, however, these missions call for specialized units and capabilities.

Combating Terrorism

As long as terrorist groups continue to target American citizens and interests, the United States will need to have specialized units available to defeat such groups. From time to time, we might also find it necessary to strike terrorists at their bases abroad or to attack assets valued by the governments that support them.

Our policy in countering international terrorists is to make no concessions to terrorists, continue to pressure state sponsors of terrorism, fully exploit all available legal mechanisms to punish international terrorists and help other governments improve their capabilities to combat terrorism.

Countering terrorism effectively requires close day-to-day coordination among Executive Branch

Engagement and Enlargement: 1995–1996 43

agencies. The Departments of State, Justice and Defense, the FBI and CIA continue to cooperate closely in an ongoing effort against international terrorists. Positive results will come from integration of intelligence, diplomatic and rule-of-law activities, and through close cooperation with other governments and international counterterrorist organizations.

Improving U.S. intelligence capacities is a significant part of the U.S. response. Terrorists, whether from well-organized groups or the kind of more loosely organized group responsible for the World Trade Center bombing, have the advantage of being able to take the initiative in the timing and choice of targets. Terrorism involving weapons of mass destruction represents a particularly dangerous potential threat that must be countered.

The United States has made concerted efforts to punish and deter terrorists. On June 26, 1993, following a determination that Iraq had plotted an assassination attempt against former President Bush, President Clinton ordered a cruise missile attack against the headquarters of Iraq's intelligence service in order to send a firm response and deter further threats. Similarly, the United States obtained convictions against defendants in the bombing of the World Trade Center.

U.S. leadership and close coordination with other governments and international bodies will continue, as demonstrated by the UN Security Council sanctions against Libya for the Pan Am 103 and UTA 772 bombings, a new international convention dealing with detecting and controlling plastic explosives, and two important counterterrorism treaties—the Protocol for the Suppression of Unlawful Acts of Violence at Airports Serving International Aviation and the Convention for the Suppression of Unlawful Attacks Against the Safety of Maritime Navigation.

Fighting Drug Trafficking

The Administration has undertaken a new approach to the global scourge of drug abuse and trafficking that will better integrate domestic and international activities to reduce both the demand and the supply of drugs. Ultimate success will depend on concerted efforts and partnerships by the public, all levels of government and the

American private sector with other governments, private groups and international bodies.

The U.S. has shifted its strategy from the past emphasis on transit interdiction to a more evenly balanced effort with source countries to build institutions, destroy trafficking organizations and stop supplies. We will support and strengthen democratic institutions abroad, denying narcotics traffickers a fragile political infrastructure in which to operate. We will also cooperate with governments that demonstrate the political will to confront the narcotics threat.

Two new comprehensive strategies have been developed, one to deal with the problem of cocaine and another to address the growing threat from high-purity heroin entering this country. We will engage more aggressively with international organizations, financial institutions and nongovernmental organizations in counternarcotics cooperation.

At home and in the international arena, prevention, treatment and economic alternatives must work hand-in-hand with law enforcement and interdiction activities. Long-term efforts will be maintained to help nations develop healthy economies with fewer market incentives for producing narcotics. The United States has increased efforts abroad to foster public awareness and support for governmental cooperation on a broad range of activities to reduce the incidence of drug abuse. Public awareness of a demand problem in producing or trafficking countries can be converted into public support and increased governmental law enforcement to reduce trafficking and production. There has been a significant attitudinal change and awareness in Latin America and the Caribbean, particularly as producer and transit nations themselves become plagued with the ill effects of consumption.

Other Missions

The United States government is also responsible for protecting the lives and safety of Americans abroad. In order to carry out this responsibility, selected U.S. military forces are trained and equipped to evacuate Americans from such situations as the outbreak of civil or international conflict and natural or man-made disasters. For example, U.S. Marines evacuated Americans from Monrovia, Liberia in August of 1990, and from Mogadishu, Somalia, in December of that year. In 1991, U.S. forces evacuated nearly 20,000 Americans from the Philippines over a three-week period following the eruption of Mount Pinatubo. Last year, U.S. Marines coupled with U.S. airlift, deployed to Burundi to help ensure the safe evacuation of U.S. citizens from ethnic fighting in Rwanda.

U.S. forces also provide invaluable training and advice to friendly governments threatened by subversion, lawlessness or insurgency. At any given time, we have small teams of military experts deployed in roughly 25 countries helping host governments cope with such challenges.

U.S. military forces and assets are frequently called upon to provide assistance to victims of floods, storms, drought and other humanitarian disasters. Both at home and abroad, U.S. forces provide emergency food, shelter, medical care and security to those in need.

Finally, the U.S. will continue as a world leader in space through its technical expertise and innovation. Over the past 30 years, as more and more nations have ventured into space, the U.S. has steadfastly recognized space as an international region. Since all nations are immediately accessible from space, the maintenance of an international legal regime for space, similar to the concept of freedom of the high seas, is especially important. Numerous attempts have been made in the past to legally limit access to space by countries that are unable, either technologically or economically, to join space-faring nations. As the commercial importance of space is developed, the U.S. can expect further pressure from non-participants to redefine the status of space, similar to what has been attempted with exclusive economic zones constraining the high seas.

Retaining the current international character of space will remain critical to achieving U.S. national security goals. Our main objectives in this area include:

- Continued freedom of access to and use of space;

- Maintaining the U.S. position as the major economic, political, military and technological power in space;

- Deterring threats to U.S. interests in space and defeating aggressive or hostile acts against U.S. space assets if deterrence fails;

- Preventing the spread of weapons of mass destruction to space;

- Enhancing global partnerships with other space-faring nations across the spectrum of economic, political and security issues.

Deciding When and How to Employ U.S. Forces

Our strategy calls for the preparation and deployment of American military forces in the United States and abroad to support U.S. diplomacy in responding to key dangers—those posed by weapons of mass destruction, regional aggression and threats to the stability of states.

Although there may be many demands for U.S. involvement, the need to husband scarce resources suggests that we must carefully select the means and level of our participation in particular military operations. And while it is unwise to specify in advance all the limitations we will place on our use of force, we must be as clear as possible about when and how we will use it.

There are three basic categories of national interests which can merit the use of our armed forces. The first involves America's vital interests, i.e., interests which are of broad, overriding importance to the survival, security and vitality of our national entity—the defense of U.S. territory, citizens, allies and economic well-being. We will do whatever it takes to defend these interests, including—when necessary—the unilateral and decisive use of military power. This was demonstrated clearly in Desert Storm and, more recently, in Vigilant Warrior.

The second category includes cases in which important, but not vital, U.S. interests are threatened. That is, the interests at stake do not affect our national survival, but they do affect importantly our national well-being and the character of the world in which we live. In such cases, military forces should only be used if they advance U.S. interests, they are likely to be able to accomplish their objectives, the costs and risks of their employment are commensurate with the interests at stake, and other means have been tried and have failed to achieve our objectives. Such uses of force should also be limited, reflecting the relative saliency of the interests we have at stake. Haiti is the most recent example in this category.

The third category involves primarily humanitarian interests. Here, our decisions focus on the resources we can bring to bear by using unique capabilities of our military rather than on the combat power of military force. Generally, the military is not the best tool to address humanitarian concerns. But under certain conditions, the use of our armed forces may be appropriate: when a humanitarian catastrophe dwarfs the ability of civilian relief agencies to respond; when the need for relief is urgent and only the military has the ability to jump-start the longer-term response to the disaster; when the response requires resources unique to the military; and when the risk to American troops is minimal. Rwanda is a good case in point. U.S. military forces performed unique and essential roles, stabilized the situation, and then got out, turning the operation over to the international relief community.

The decision on *whether and when* to use force is therefore dictated first and foremost by our national interests. In those specific areas where our vital or survival interests are at stake, our use of force will be decisive and, if necessary, unilateral. In other situations posing a less immediate threat, our military engagement must be targeted selectively on those areas that most affect our national interests—for instance, areas where we have a sizable economic stake or commitments to allies, and areas where there is a potential to generate substantial refugee flows into our nation or our allies.

Second, in all cases the costs and risks of U.S. military involvement must be judged to be commensurate with the stakes involved. We will be more inclined to act where there is reason to believe that our action will bring lasting improvement. On the other hand, our involvement will be more circumscribed when other regional or multilateral actors are better positioned to act than we are. Even in these cases, however, the United States will be actively engaged at the diplomatic level. In every case, however, we will consider several critical questions before committing military force: Have we considered non-military means that offer a reasonable chance of success? Is there a clearly defined, achievable mission? What is the environment of risk we are entering? What is needed to achieve our goals? What are the potential costs—both human and financial—of the engagement? Do we have reasonable assurance of support from the American people and their elected representatives? Do we have timeliness and milestones that will reveal the extent of success or failure, and, in either case, do we have an exit strategy?

The decision on *how* we use force has a similar set of derived guidelines:

First, when we send American troops abroad, we will send them with a clear mission and, for those operations that are likely to involve combat, the means to achieve their objectives decisively, having answered the questions: What types of U.S. military capabilities should be brought to bear, and is the use of military force carefully matched to our political objectives?

Second, as much as possible, we will seek the help of our allies and friends or of relevant international institutions. If our most important national interests are at stake, we are prepared to act alone. But especially on those matters touching directly the interests of our allies, there should be a proportionate commitment from them. Working together increases the effectiveness of each nation's actions, and sharing the responsibilities lessens everyone's load.

These, then, are the calculations of interest and cost that have influenced our past uses of military power and will guide us in the future. Every time this Administration has used force, it has balanced interests against costs. And in each case, the use of our military has put power behind our diplomacy, allowing us to make progress we would not otherwise have achieved.

One final consideration regards the central role the American people rightfully play in how the United States wields its power abroad: the United States cannot long sustain a fight without the support of the public. This is true for humanitarian and other non-traditional interventions, as well as war. Modern media communications confront every American with images which both stir the impulse to intervene and raise the question of an operation's costs and risks. When it is judged in America's interest to intervene, we must use force with an unwavering commitment to our objective. While we must continue to reassess any operation's costs and benefits as it unfolds and the full range of our options, reflexive calls for early withdrawal of our forces as soon as casualties arise endangers our objectives as well as our troops. Doing so invites any rogue actor to attack our troops to try to force our departure from areas where our interests lie.

Combating the Spread and Use of Weapons of Mass Destruction and Missiles

Weapons of mass destruction—nuclear, biological and chemical—along with their associated delivery systems, pose a major threat to our security and that of our allies and other friendly nations. Thus, a key part of our strategy is to seek to stem the proliferation of such weapons and to develop an effective capability to deal with these threats. We also need to maintain robust strategic nuclear forces and seek to implement existing strategic arms agreements.

Nonproliferation and Counterproliferation

A critical priority for the United States is to stem the proliferation of nuclear weapons and other weapons of mass destruction and their missile delivery systems. Countries' weapons programs, and their levels of cooperation with our nonproliferation efforts, will be among our most important criteria in judging the nature of our bilateral relations.

soon as possible, ending the unsafeguarded production of fissile materials for nuclear weapons purposes and strengthening the Nuclear Suppliers Group and the International Atomic Energy Agency (IAEA) are important goals. They complement our comprehensive efforts to discourage the accumulation of fissile materials, to seek to strengthen controls and constraints on those materials, and over time, to reduce worldwide stocks. As President Clinton announced at last September's UN General Assembly, we will seek a global ban on the production of fissile material for nuclear weapons.

To combat missile proliferation, the United States seeks prudently to broaden membership of the Missile Technology Control Regime (MTCR). The Administration supports the earliest possible ratification and entry in force of the Chemical Weapons Convention (CWC) as well as new measures to deter violations of and enhance compliance with the Biological Weapons Convention (BWC). We also support improved export controls for nonproliferation purposes both domestically and multilaterally.

Through programs such as the Nunn-Lugar Cooperative Threat Reduction effort and other denuclearization initiatives, important progress has been made to build a more secure international environment. One striking example was the successful transfer last fall of nearly six hundred kilograms of vulnerable nuclear material from Kazakhstan to safe storage in the United States. Kazakhstan was concerned about the security of the material and requested U.S. assistance in removing it to safe storage. The Departments of Defense and Energy undertook a joint mission to retrieve the uranium. Similarly, under an agreement we secured with Russia, it is converting tons of highly-enriched uranium from dismantled weapons into commercial reactor fuel for purchase by the United States. The United States is also working with Russia to enhance control and accounting of nuclear material.

As a key part of our effort to control nuclear proliferation, we seek the indefinite and unconditional extension of the Nuclear Nonproliferation Treaty (NPT) and its universal application. Achieving a Comprehensive Test Ban Treaty as

The proliferation problem is global, but we must tailor our approaches to specific regional contexts. We have concluded an agreed framework to bring North Korea into full compliance with its nonproliferation obligations, including the NPT and IAEA safeguards. We will continue efforts to prevent Iran from advancing its weapons of mass destruction objectives and to thwart Iraq from reconstituting its previous programs. The United States seeks to cap, reduce and, ultimately, eliminate the nuclear and missile capabilities of India and Pakistan. In the Middle East and elsewhere, we encourage regional arms control agreements that address the legitimate security concerns of all parties. These tasks are being pursued with other states that share our concern for the enormous challenge of stemming the proliferation of such weapons.

The United States has signed bilateral agreements with Russia, Ukraine and South Africa which commit these countries to adhere to the guidelines of the MTCR. We also secured China's commitment to observe the MTCR guidelines and its agreement not to transfer MTCR-controlled ground-to-ground missiles. Russia has agreed not to transfer space-launch vehicle technology with potential military applications to India. South Africa has agreed to observe the MTCR guidelines and to dismantle its Category I missile systems and has joined the NPT and accepted full-scope safeguards. Hungary, the Czech Republic, the Slovak Republic and Poland have joined the Australia Group (which controls the transfer of items that could be used to make chemical or biological weapons). Hungary and Argentina have joined the MTCR and Brazil has committed itself publicly to adhere to the MTCR guidelines. Argentina, Brazil and Chile have brought the Treaty of Tlatelolco into force. We continue to push for the dismantlement of all intercontinental ballistic missiles located in Ukraine and Kazakhstan. With the United States and Russia, Ukraine is pressing forward on implementation of the Trilateral Statement, which provides for the transfer of all nuclear warheads from Ukraine to Russia for dismantlement in return for fair compensation.

Thus, the United States seeks to prevent additional countries from acquiring chemical, biological and nuclear weapons and the means to deliver them. However, should such efforts fail, U.S. forces must be prepared to deter, prevent and defend against their use. As agreed at the January 1994 NATO Summit, we are working with our Allies to develop a policy framework to consider how to reinforce ongoing prevention efforts and to reduce the proliferation threat and protect against it.

The United States will retain the capacity to retaliate against those who might contemplate the use of weapons of mass destruction, so that the costs of such use will be seen as outweighing the gains. However, to minimize the impact of proliferation of weapons of mass destruction on our interests, we will need the capability not only to deter their use against either ourselves or our allies and friends, but also, where necessary and feasible, to prevent it.

This will require improved defensive capabilities. To minimize the vulnerability of our forces abroad to weapons of mass destruction, we are placing a high priority on improving our ability to locate, identify and disable arsenals of weapons of

Nuclear Forces

In September, the President approved the recommendations of the Pentagon's Nuclear Posture Review (NPR). A key conclusion of this review is that the United States will retain a triad of strategic nuclear forces sufficient to deter any future hostile foreign leadership with access to strategic nuclear forces from acting against our vital interests and to convince it that seeking a nuclear advantage would be futile. Therefore, we will continue to maintain nuclear forces of sufficient size and capability to hold at risk a broad range of assets valued by such political and military leaders. The President approved the NPR's recommended strategic nuclear force posture as the U.S. START II force. The forces are: 450–500 Minuteman ICBMs, 14 Trident submarines all with D-5 missiles, 20 B-2 and 66 B-52 strategic bombers, and a non-nuclear role for the B-1s. This force posture allows us the flexibility to reconstitute or reduce further, as conditions warrant. The NPR also reaffirmed the current posture and deployment of non-strategic nuclear forces; the United States will eliminate carrier and surface ship nuclear weapons capability.

Arms Control

Arms control is an integral part of our national security strategy. Arms control can help reduce incentives to initiate attack; enhance predictability regarding the size and structure of forces, thus reducing fear of aggressive intent; reduce the size of national defense industry establishments and thus permit the growth of more vital, nonmilitary industries; ensure confidence in compliance through effective monitoring and verification; and, ultimately, contribute to a more stable and calculable balance of power.

In the area of strategic arms control, prescribed reductions in strategic offensive arms and the steady shift toward less destabilizing systems remain indispensable. Ukraine's accession to the Nuclear Nonproliferation Treaty—joining

Belarus's and Kazakhstan's decision to be non-nuclear nations—was followed immediately by the exchange of instruments of ratification and brought the START I treaty into force at the December CSCE summit, paving the way for ratification of the START II Treaty. Under START II, the United States and Russia will each be left with between 3,000 and 3,500 deployed strategic nuclear warheads, which is a two-thirds reduction from the Cold War peak. The two Presidents agreed that once START II is ratified, both nations will immediately begin to deactivate or otherwise remove from combat status, those systems whose elimination will be required by that treaty, rather than waiting for the treaty to run its course through the year 2003. START II ratification will also open the door to the next round of strategic arms control, in which we will consider what further reductions in, or limitations on, remaining U.S. and Russian nuclear forces should be carried out. We will also explore strategic confidence-building measures and mutual understandings that reduce the risk of accidental war.

The full and faithful implementation of other existing arms control agreements, including the Anti-Ballistic Missile (ABM) Treaty, Strategic Arms Reduction Talks I (START I), Biological Weapons Convention (BWC), Intermediate-range Nuclear Forces (INF) Treaty, Conventional Forces in Europe (CFE) Treaty, several nuclear testing agreements, the 1994 Vienna Document on Confidence and Security-Building Measures (CSBMs), Open Skies, the Environmental Modification Convention (EnMod), Incidents at Sea and many others will remain an important element of national security policy. The ongoing negotiation initiated by the United States to clarify the ABM Treaty by establishing an agreed demarcation between strategic and theater ballistic missiles and update the Treaty to reflect the break-up of the Soviet Union reflects the Administration's commitment to maintaining the integrity and effectiveness of crucial arms control agreements.

Future arms control efforts may become more regional and multilateral. Regional arrangements can add predictability and openness to security relations, advance the rule of international law and promote cooperation among participants. They help maintain deterrence and a stable military balance at regional levels. The U.S. is prepared to promote, help negotiate, monitor and participate in regional arms control undertakings compatible with American national security interests. We will generally support such undertakings but will not seek to impose regional arms control accords against the wishes of affected states.

As arms control, whether regional or global, becomes increasingly multilateral, the Conference on Disarmament (CD) in Geneva will play an even more important role. The U.S. will support measures to increase the effectiveness and relevance of the CD. Arms control agreements can head off potential arms races in certain weapons categories or in some environments. We will continue to seek greater transparency, responsibility and, where appropriate, restraint in the transfer of conventional weapons and global military spending. The UN register of conventional arms transfers is a start in promoting greater transparency of weapons transfers and buildups, but more needs to be done. The U.S. has proposed that the new regime to succeed the Coordinating Committee (COCOM) focus on conventional arms sales and dual-use technologies. Where appropriate, the United States will continue to pursue such efforts vigorously. Measures to reduce oversized defense industrial establishments, especially those parts involved with weapons of mass destruction, will also contribute to stability in the post–Cold War world. The Administration also will pursue defense conversion agreements with the Former Soviet Union (FSU) states, and defense conversion is also on the agenda with China. The United States has also proposed a regime to reduce the number and availability of the world's long-lived antipersonnel mines whose indiscriminate and irresponsible use has reached crisis proportions. As another part of our effort to address this landmine problem, the Administration has also submitted the Convention on Conventional Weapons to the Senate for advice and consent.

Peace Operations

In addition to preparing for major regional contingencies, we must prepare our forces for peace operations to support democracy or conflict resolution. The United States, along with others in the international community, will seek to prevent and contain localized conflicts before they require a military response. U.S. support capabilities such as airlift, intelligence and global communications, have often contributed to the success of multilateral peace operations, and they will continue to do so. U.S. combat units are less likely to be used for most peace operations, but in some cases their use will be necessary or desirable and justified by U.S. national interests as guided by the Presidential Decision Directive, "U.S. Policy on Reforming Multilateral Peace Operations," and outlined below.

Multilateral peace operations are an important component of our strategy. From traditional peacekeeping to peace enforcement, multilateral peace operations are sometimes the best way to prevent, contain, or.resolve conflicts that could otherwise be far more costly and deadly.

Engagement and Enlargement: 1995–1996 69

Peace operations often have served, and continue to serve, important U.S. national interests. In some cases, they have helped preserve peace between nations, as in Cyprus and the Golan Heights. In others, peacekeepers have provided breathing room for fledgling democracies, as in Cambodia, El Salvador and Namibia.

At the same time, however, we must recognize that some types of peace operations make demands on the UN that exceed the organization's current capabilities. The United States is working with the UN headquarters and other member states to ensure that the UN embarks only on peace operations that make political and military sense and that the UN is able to manage effectively those peace operations it does undertake. We support the creation of a professional UN peace operations headquarters with a planning staff, access to timely intelligence, a logistics unit that can be rapidly deployed and a modern operations center with global communications. The United States will reduce our peacekeeping payments to 25 percent while working to ensure that other nations pay their fair share. We are also working to ensure that peacekeeping operations by appropriate regional organizations such as NATO and the OSCE can be carried out effectively.

In order to maximize the benefits of UN peace operations, the United States must make highly disciplined choices about when and under what circumstances to support or participate in them. The need to exercise such discipline is at the heart of President Clinton's policy on Reforming Multilateral Peace Operations. Far from handing a blank check to the UN, the President's policy review on peace operations—the most thorough ever undertaken by an Administration—requires the United States to undertake a rigorous analysis of requirements and capabilities before voting to support or participate in peace operations. The United States has not hesitated to use its position on the Security Council to ensure that the UN authorizes only those peace operations that meet these standards.

Most UN peacekeeping operations do not involve U.S. forces. On those occasions when we consider contributing U.S. forces to a UN peace operation, we will employ rigorous criteria, including the same principles that would guide any decision to employ U.S. forces. In addition, we will ensure that the risks to U.S. personnel and the command and control arrangements governing the participation of American and foreign forces are acceptable to the United States.

The question of command and control is particularly critical. There may be times when it is in our interest to place U.S. troops under the temporary operational control of a competent UN or allied commander. The United States has done so many times in the past—from the siege of Yorktown in the Revolutionary War to the battles of Desert Storm. However, under no circumstances will the President ever relinquish his command authority over U.S. forces.

Improving the ways the United States and the UN decide upon and conduct peace operations will not make the decision to engage any easier. The lesson we must take away from our first ventures in peace operations is not that we should forswear such operations but that we should employ this tool selectively and more effectively. In short, the United States views peace operations as a means to support our national security strategy, not as a strategy unto itself.

The President is firmly committed to securing the active support of the Congress for U.S. participation in peace operations. The Administration has set forth a detailed blueprint to guide consultations with Congress. With respect to particular operations, the Administration will undertake consultations on questions such as the nature of expected U.S. military participation, the mission parameters of the operation, the expected duration and budgetary implications. In addition to such operation-specific consultations, the Administration has also conducted regular monthly briefings for congressional staff, and will deliver an Annual Comprehensive Report to Congress on Peace Operations. Congress is critical to the institutional development of a successful U.S. policy on peace operations, including the resolution of funding issues which have an impact on military readiness.

Two other points deserve emphasis. First, the primary mission of our Armed Forces is not peace operations; it is to deter and, if necessary, to fight and win conflicts in which our most important interests are threatened. Second, while the international community can create conditions for peace, the responsibility for peace ultimately rests with the people of the country in question.

Strong Intelligence Capabilities

U.S. intelligence capabilities are critical instruments of our national power and remain an integral part of our national security strategy. Only a strong intelligence effort can provide adequate warning of threats to U.S. national security and identify opportunities for advancing our interests. Policy analysts, decision makers and military commanders at all levels will continue to rely on our intelligence community to collect information unavailable from other sources and to provide strategic and tactical analysis to help surmount potential challenges to our military, political and economic interests.

Because national security has taken on a much broader definition in this post–Cold War era, intelligence must address a much wider range of threats and dangers. We will continue to monitor military and technical threats, to guide long-term force development and weapons acquisition, and to directly support military operations. Intelligence will also be critical for directing new efforts against regional conflicts, proliferation of WMD, counterintelligence, terrorism and narcotics trafficking. In order to adequately forecast dangers to democracy and to U.S. economic well-being, the intelligence community must track political, economic, social and military developments in those parts of the world where U.S. interests are most heavily engaged and where overt collection of information from open sources is inadequate. Finally, to enhance the study and support of worldwide environmental, humanitarian and disaster relief activities, technical intelligence assets (principally imagery) must be directed to a greater degree toward collection of data on these subjects.

The collection and analysis of intelligence related to economic development will play an increasingly important role in helping policy makers understand economic trends. That collection and analysis can help level the economic playing field by identifying threats to U.S. companies from foreign intelligence services and unfair trading practices.

This strategy requires that we take steps to reinforce current intelligence capabilities and overt foreign service reporting, within the limits of our resources, and similar steps to enhance coordination of clandestine and overt collection. Key goals include to:

- Provide timely warning of strategic threats, whether from the remaining arsenal of weapons in the former Soviet Union or from other nations with weapons of mass destruction;

- Ensure timely intelligence support to military operations;

- Provide early warning of potential crises and facilitate preventive diplomacy;

- Develop new strategies for collection, production and dissemination (including closer relationships between intelligence producers and consumers) to make intelligence products more responsive to current consumer needs;

- Improve worldwide technical capabilities to detect, identify and determine the efforts of foreign nations to develop weapons of mass destruction;

- Enhance counterintelligence capabilities;

- Provide focused support for law enforcement agencies in areas like counternarcotics, counterterrorism and illegal technology trade;

- Streamline intelligence operations and organizations to gain efficiency and integration;

- Revise long-standing security restrictions where possible to make intelligence data more useful to intelligence consumers.

- Develop security countermeasures based on sound threat analysis and risk management practices

To advance these goals the President significantly restructured counterintelligence policy development and interagency coordination. In a Presidential Decision Directive (PDD) on U.S. counterintelligence effectiveness, the President took immediate steps to improve our ability to counter both traditional and new threats to our Nation's security in the post–Cold War era. The President further directed a comprehensive restructuring of the process by which our security policies, practices and procedures are developed and implemented. The PDD on Security Policy Coordination ensures the development of security policies and practices that realistically meet the threats we face as they continue to evolve, at a price we can afford, while guaranteeing the fair and equitable treatment of all Americans upon whom we rely to guard our nation's security. Consistent with the provisions of the FY 1995 Intelligence Authorization Act, President Clinton has also directed the Chairman of the Foreign Intelligence Advisory Board to conduct a comprehensive review of the roles and missions of the intelligence community and fundamentally evaluate and define the need for intelligence in the post–Cold War environment.

The Environment and Sustainable Development

The more clearly we understand the complex interrelationships between the different parts of our world's environment, the better we can understand the regional and even global effects of local changes to the environment. Increasing competition for the dwindling reserves of uncontaminated air, arable land, fisheries and other food sources, and water, once considered "free" goods, is already a very real risk to regional stability around the world. The range of environmental risks serious enough to jeopardize international stability extends to massive population flight from manmade or natural catastrophes, such as Chernobyl or the East African drought, and to large-scale ecosystem damage caused by industrial pollution, deforestation, loss of biodiversity, ozone depletion, desertification, ocean pollution and ultimately climate change. Strategies dealing with environmental issues of this magnitude will require partnerships between governments and nongovernmental organizations, cooperation between nations and regions, and a commitment to a strategically focused, long-term policy for emerging environmental risks.

The decisions we make today regarding military force structures typically influence our ability to respond to threats 20 to 30 years in the future. Similarly, our current decisions regarding the environment and natural resources will affect the magnitude of their security risks over at least a comparable period of time, if not longer. The measure of our difficulties in the future will be settled by the steps we take in the present.

As a priority initiative, the U.S. successfully led efforts at the September Cairo Conference to develop a consensus Program of Action to address the continuous climb in global population, including increased availability of family planning and reproductive health services, sustainable economic development, the empowerment of women to include enhanced educational opportunities and a reduction in infant and child mortality. Rapid population growth in the developing world and unsustainable consumption patterns in industrialized nations are the root of both present and potentially even greater forms of environmental degradation and resource depletion. A conservative estimate of the globe's population projects 8.5 billion people on the planet by the year 2025. Even when making the most generous allowances for advances in science and technology, one cannot help but conclude that population growth and environmental pressures will feed into immense social unrest and make the world substantially more vulnerable to serious international frictions.

Promoting Prosperity at Home

A central goal of our national security strategy is to promote America's prosperity through efforts both at home and abroad. Our economic and security interests are increasingly inseparable. Our prosperity at home depends on engaging actively abroad. The strength of our diplomacy, our ability to maintain an unrivaled military, the attractiveness of our values abroad—all these depend in part on the strength of our economy.

Enhancing American Competitiveness

Our primary economic goal is to strengthen the American economy. The first step toward that goal was reducing the federal deficit and the burden it imposes on the economy and future generations. The economic program passed in 1993 has restored investor confidence in the U.S. and strengthened our position in international economic negotiations. Under the Clinton economic plan, the deficit will be reduced over 700 billion dollars by Fiscal Year 1998. President Clinton has also lowered the deficit as a percentage of the Gross Domestic Product from 4.9 percent in Fiscal Year 1992 to 2.4 percent in Fiscal Year 1995—the lowest since 1979.

And Fiscal Year 1995 will be the first time that the deficit has been reduced three years in a row since the Truman Administration. We are building on this deficit reduction effort with other steps to improve American competitiveness: investing in science and technology; assisting defense conversion; improving information networks and other vital infrastructure; and improving education and training programs for America's workforce. We are structuring our defense R&D effort to place greater emphasis on dual-use technologies that can enhance competitiveness and meet pressing military needs. We are also reforming the defense acquisition system so that we can develop and procure weapons and materiel more efficiently.

Partnership with Business and Labor

Our economic strategy views the private sector as the engine of economic growth. It sees government's role as a partner to the private sector—acting as an advocate of U.S. business interests; leveling the playing field in international markets; helping to boost American exports; and finding ways to remove domestic and foreign barriers to the creativity, initiative and productivity of American business.

To this end, on September 29, 1993, the Administration published its report creating

America's first national export strategy and making 65 specific recommendations for reforming the way government works with the private sector to expand exports. Among the recommendations were significant improvements in advocacy, export financing, market information systems and product standards education. The results of these reforms could enable U.S. exports to reach the trillion dollar mark by the turn of the century, which would help create at least six million new American jobs.

Another critical element in boosting U.S. exports is reforming the outdated export licensing system. That reform began with significant liberalization of export licensing controls for computers, supercomputers and telecommunications equipment. The Administration is also seeking comprehensive reform of the Export Administration Act, which governs the process of export licensing. The goal of this reform is to strengthen our ability to prevent proliferation and protect other national interests, while removing unnecessarily burdensome licensing requirements left over from the Cold War.

Enhancing Access to Foreign Markets

The success of American business is more than ever dependent upon success in international markets. The ability to compete internationally also assures that our companies will continue to innovate and increase productivity, which will in turn lead to improvements in our own living standards. But to compete abroad, our firms need access to foreign markets, just as foreign industries have access to our open market. We vigorously pursue measures to increase access for our companies—through bilateral, regional and multilateral arrangements.

The North American Free Trade Agreement

On December 3, 1993, President Clinton signed the North American Free Trade Act (NAFTA), which creates a free trade zone among the United States, Canada and Mexico. NAFTA has already created more than 100,000 American jobs. NAFTA has increased Mexico's capacity to cooperate with our nation on a wide range of issues that cross our 2,000-mile border—including the environment, narcotics trafficking and illegal immigration.

ASIA-PACIFIC ECONOMIC COOPERATION

Our economic relations depend vitally on our ties with the Asia-Pacific region, which is the world's fastest-growing economic region. In November 1993, President Clinton convened the first-ever summit of the leaders of the economies that constitute the Asia-Pacific Economic Cooperation (APEC) forum. U.S. initiatives in the APEC forum will open new opportunities for economic cooperation and permit U.S. companies to become involved in substantial infrastructure planning and construction throughout the region. The trade and investment framework agreed to in 1993 provided the basis for enhancing the "open regionalism" that defines APEC. At the second leaders meeting in November 1994, the leaders of APEC further drove the process by accepting the goal of free and open trade and investment throughout the region by early in the 21st century, and agreeing to lay out a blueprint for achieving that goal by the Osaka APEC leaders meeting.

Uruguay Round of GATT

The successful conclusion in December 1993 of the Uruguay Round of the negotiations under the General Agreement on Tariffs and Trade (GATT) significantly strengthened the world trading system. The Uruguay Round accord is the largest, most comprehensive trade agreement in history. It will create hundreds of thousands of new U.S. jobs and expand opportunities for U.S. businesses. For the first time, international trade rules will apply to services, intellectual property and investments, and effective rules will apply to agriculture. The Uruguay Round also continued the cuts in tariff rates throughout the world that began just after the Second World War. Working with Congress, the President secured U.S. approval of this path-breaking agreement and the resulting World Trade Organization which provides a forum to resolve disputes openly. The President remains committed to ensuring that the commitments in the Uruguay Round agreement are fulfilled.

U.S.-Japan Framework Agreement

While Japan is America's second-largest export market, foreign access to the Japanese market remains limited in important sectors, including automobiles and automobile parts. Japan's persistent current account surpluses are a major imbalance in the global economy. In July 1993 President Clinton and Japanese Prime Minister Miyazawa established the U.S.-Japan Framework for Economic Partnership to redress the imbalances in our economic relationship. In October 1994, the United States and Japan reached framework agreements regarding government procurement of medical technologies and telecommunications (including Nippon Telephone and Telegraph [NPP] procurement). In December, we concluded a further agreement on flat glass. We have also reached framework agreements on financial services and intellectual property rights. The Administration is committed to ensuring that competitive American goods and services have fair access to the Japanese market. We will continue to work to ensure that Japan takes measures to open its markets and stimulate its economy, both to benefit its own people and to fulfill its international responsibilities.

Summit of the Americas

America's economy benefits enormously from the opportunity offered by the commitment of the democratic nations of the Western Hemisphere to negotiate a free trade agreement for the region by 2005. The Western Hemisphere is our largest export market, constituting over 35 percent of all U.S. sales abroad. The action plan will accelerate progress toward free, integrated markets which will create new high-wage jobs and sustain economic growth for America. The invitation to Chile to begin negotiations to join NAFTA is the first step toward the Summit's goal of reaching a hemispheric free trade zone.

Expanding the Realm of Free Trade

The conclusion of NAFTA, the Uruguay Round, the Bogor Declaration of the 1994 APEC leaders meeting, and the Summit of the Americas' action plan represents unprecedented progress toward more open markets both at the regional and global levels. The Administration intends to continue its efforts in further enhancing U.S. access to foreign markets. The World Trade Organization will provide a new institutional lever for securing such access. Emerging markets, particularly along the Pacific Rim, present vast opportunities for American enterprise, and APEC now provides a suitable vehicle for the exploration of such opportunities. Similarly, the United States convened the Summit of the Americas to seize the opportunities created by the movement toward open markets throughout the hemisphere. All such steps in the direction of expanded trading relationships will be undertaken in a way consistent with protection of the international environment and to the goal of sustainable development here and abroad.

Strengthening Macroeconomic Coordination

As national economies become more integrated internationally, the U.S. cannot thrive in isolation from developments abroad. International economic expansion is benefiting from G-7 macroeconomic policy coordination. To improve global macroeconomic performance, we will continue to work through the G-7 process to promote growth-oriented policies to complement our own efforts.

Providing for Energy Security

The United States depends on oil for more than 40 percent of its primary energy needs. Roughly 45 percent of our oil needs are met with imports, and a large share of these imports come from the Persian Gulf area. The experiences of the two oil shocks and the Gulf War show that an interruption of oil supplies can have a significant impact on the economies of the United States and its allies. Appropriate economic responses can substantially mitigate the balance of payments and inflationary impacts of an oil shock; appropriate foreign policy responses to events such as Iraq's invasion of Kuwait can limit the magnitude of the crisis.

Over the longer term, the United States' dependence on access to foreign oil sources will be increasingly important as our resources are depleted. The U.S. economy has grown roughly 75 percent since the first oil shock; yet during that time our oil consumption has remained virtually stable and oil production has declined. High oil prices did not generate enough new oil exploration and discovery to sustain production levels from our depleted resource base. These facts show the need for continued and extended reliance on energy efficiency and conservation and development of alternative energy sources. Conservation measures notwithstanding, the U.S. has a vital interest in unrestricted access to this critical resource.

Promoting Sustainable Development Abroad

Broad-based economic development not only improves the prospects for democratic development in developing countries, but also expands the demands for U.S. exports. Economic growth abroad can alleviate pressure on the global environment, reduce the attraction of illegal narcotics trade and improve the health and economic productivity of global populations.

The environmental aspects of ill-designed economic growth are clear. Environmental damage will ultimately block economic growth. Rapid urbanization is outstripping the ability of nations to provide jobs, education and other services to new citizens. The continuing poverty of a quarter of the world's people leads to hunger, malnutrition, economic migration and political unrest. Widespread illiteracy and lack of technical skills hinder employment opportunities and drive entire populations to support themselves on increasingly fragile and damaged resource bases. New diseases such as AIDS and epidemics, often spread through environmental degradation, threaten to overwhelm the health facilities of developing countries, disrupt societies and stop economic growth. These realities must be addressed by sustainable development programs which offer viable alternatives. U.S. leadership is of the essence. If such alternatives are not developed, the consequences for the planet's future will be grave indeed.

Domestically, the U.S. must work hard to halt local and cross-border environmental degradation.

In addition, the U.S. should foster environmental technology targeting pollution prevention, control and cleanup. Companies that invest in energy efficiency, clean manufacturing and environmental services today will create the high-quality, high-wage jobs of tomorrow. By providing access to these types of technologies, our exports can also provide the means for other nations to achieve environmentally sustainable economic growth. At the same time, we are taking ambitious steps at home to better manage our natural resources and reduce energy and other consumption, decrease waste generation and increase our recycling efforts.

Internationally, the Administration's foreign assistance program focuses on four key elements of sustainable development: broad-based economic growth; the environment; population and health; and democracy. We will continue to advocate environmentally sound private investment and responsible approaches by international lenders. At our urging, the Multilateral Development Banks (MDB's) are now placing increased emphasis upon sustainable development in their funding decisions, to include a commitment to perform environmental assessments on projects for both internal and public scrutiny. In particular, the Global Environmental Facility (GEF), established last year, will provide a source of financial assistance to the developing world for climate change, biodiversity and oceans initiatives.

The U.S. is taking specific steps now in all of these areas:

- In June 1993, the United States signed the Convention on Biological Diversity, which aims to protect and utilize the world's genetic inheritance. The Interior Department has been directed to create a national biological survey to help protect species and to help the agricultural and biotechnical industries identify new sources of food, fiber and medications.

- New policies are being implemented to ensure the sustainable management of U.S. forests by the year 2000, as pledged internationally. In addition, U.S. bilateral forest assistance programs are being expanded, and the United States is promoting sustainable management of tropical forests.

- In the wake of the 1992 United Nations Conference on Environment and Development, the United States has sought to reduce land-based sources of marine pollution, maintain populations of marine species at healthy and productive levels and protect endangered marine mammals.

- The United States has focused technical assistance and encouraged nongovernmental environmental groups to provide expertise to the republics of the Former Soviet Union and Central and Eastern European nations that have suffered the most acute environmental crises. The Agency for International Development, the Environmental Protection Agency and other U.S. agencies are engaged in technical cooperation with many countries around the world to advance these goals.

- The Administration is leading a renewed global effort to address population problems and promote international consensus for stabilizing world population growth. Our comprehensive approach will stress family planning and reproductive health care, maternal and child health, education and improving the status of women. The International Conference on Population Development, held in September in Cairo, endorsed these approaches as important strategies in achieving our global population goals.

Promoting Democracy

All of America's strategic interests—from promoting prosperity at home to checking global threats abroad before they threaten our territory—are served by enlarging the community of democratic and free market nations. Thus, working with new democratic states to help preserve them as democracies committed to free markets and respect for human rights, is a key part of our national security strategy.

One of the most gratifying and encouraging developments of the past 15 years is the explosion in the number of states moving away from repressive governance and toward democracy. Since the success of many of those experiments is by no means assured, our strategy of enlargement must focus on the consolidation of those regimes and the broadening of their commitment to democracy. At the same time, we seek to increase respect for fundamental human rights in all states and encourage an evolution to democracy where that is possible.

The enlargement of the community of market democracies respecting human rights and the environment is manifest in a number of ways:

- More than 30 nations in Central and Eastern Europe, the former Soviet Union, Latin America, Africa and East Asia have, over the past 10 years, adopted the structures of a constitutional democracy and held free elections;

- The nations of the Western Hemisphere have proclaimed their commitment to democratic regimes and to the collective responsibility of the nations of the OAS to respond to threats to democracy.

- In the Western Hemisphere, only Cuba is not a democratic state.

- Nations as diverse as South Africa, Cambodia and El Salvador have resolved bitter internal disputes with agreement on the creation of constitutional democracies.

The first element of our democracy strategy is to work with the other democracies of the world and to improve our cooperation with them on security and economic issues. We also seek their support in enlarging the realm of democratic nations.

The core of our strategy is to help democracy and markets expand and survive in other places where we have the strongest security concerns and where we can make the greatest difference. This is not a democratic crusade; it is a pragmatic commitment to see freedom take hold where that will

Engagement and Enlargement: 1995–1996

help us most. Thus, we must target our effort to assist states that affect our strategic interests, such as those with large economies, critical locations, nuclear weapons or the potential to generate refugee flows into our own nation or into key friends and allies. We must focus our efforts where we have the most leverage. And our efforts must be demand-driven—they must focus on nations whose people are pushing for reform or have already secured it.

Russia is a key state in this regard. If we can support and help consolidate democratic and market reforms in Russia (and the other newly independent states), we can help turn a former threat into a region of valued diplomatic and economic partners. Our intensified interaction with Ukraine has helped move that country on to the path of economic reform, which is critical to its long-term stability. In addition, our efforts in Russia, Ukraine and the other states support and facilitate our efforts to achieve continued reductions in nuclear arms and compliance with international nonproliferation accords.

The new democracies in Central and Eastern Europe are another clear example, given their proximity to the great democratic powers of Western Europe, their importance to our security and their potential markets.

Since our ties across the Pacific are no less important than those across the Atlantic, pursuing enlargement in the Asian Pacific is a third example. We will work to support the emerging democracies of the region and to encourage other states along the same path.

Continuing the great strides toward democracy and markets in our hemisphere is also a key concern and was behind the President's decision to host the Summit of the Americas in December 1994. As we continue such efforts, we should be on the lookout for states whose entry into the camp of market democracies may influence the future direction of an entire region; South Africa now holds that potential with regard to sub-Saharan Africa.

How should the United States help consolidate and enlarge democracy and markets in these states? The answers are as varied as the nations involved, but there are common elements. We must continue to help lead the effort to mobilize international resources, as we have with Russia, Ukraine and the other new independent states. We must be willing to take immediate public positions to help staunch democratic reversals, as we have in Haiti and Guatemala. We must give democratic nations the fullest benefits of integration into foreign markets, which is part of why NAFTA and the GATT ranked so high on our agenda. And we must help these nations strengthen the pillars of civil society, improve their market institutions, and fight corruption and political discontent through practices of good governance.

At the same time as we work to ensure the success of emerging democracies, we must also redouble our efforts to guarantee basic human rights on a global basis. At the 1993 United Nations Conference on Human Rights, the United States forcefully and successfully argued for a reaffirmation of the universality of such rights and improved international mechanisms for their promotion. In the wake of this gathering, the UN has named a High Commissioner for Human Rights, and the rights of women have been afforded a new international precedence. The United States has taken the lead in assisting the UN to set up international tribunals to enforce accountability for the war crimes in the former Yugoslavia and in Rwanda.

The United States also continues to work for the protection of human rights on a bilateral basis. To demonstrate our own willingness to adhere to international human rights standards, the United States ratified the international convention prohibiting discrimination on the basis of race, and the Administration is seeking Senate consent to ratification for the convention prohibiting discrimination against women. The United States will play a major role in promoting women's rights internationally at the UN Women's Conference in September.

In all these efforts, a policy of engagement and enlargement should take on a second meaning: we should pursue our goals through an enlarged circle not only of government officials but also of private and non-governmental groups. Private firms are natural allies in our efforts to strengthen market economies. Similarly, our goal of strengthening democracy and civil society has a natural ally in labor unions, human rights groups, environmental advocates, chambers of commerce and election monitors. Just as we rely on force multipliers in defense, we should welcome these "diplomacy multipliers," such as the National Endowment for Democracy.

Supporting the global movement toward democracy requires a pragmatic and long-term effort focused on both values and institutions. The United States must build on the opportunities achieved through the successful conclusion of the Cold War. Our long-term goal is a world in which each of the major powers is democratic, with many other nations joining the community of market democracies as well.

Our efforts to promote democracy and human rights are complemented by our humanitarian assistance programs which are designed to alleviate human suffering and to pave the way for progress toward establishing democratic regimes with a commitment to respect for human rights and appropriate strategies for economic development. We are also exploring ideas such as the suggestion of Argentina's President Menem for the creation of an international civilian rapid response capability for humanitarian crises, including a school and training for humanitarian operations.

Through humanitarian assistance and policy initiatives aimed at the sources of disruption, we seek to mitigate the contemporary migration and refugee crises, foster long-term global cooperation and strengthen involved international institutions. The U.S. will provide appropriate financial support and will work with other nations and international bodies, such as the International Red Cross and the UN High Commissioner for Refugees, in seeking voluntary repatriation of refugees—taking into full consideration human rights concerns as well as the economic conditions that may have driven them out in the first place. Helping refugees return to their homes in Mozambique, Afghanistan, Eritrea, Somalia and Guatemala, for example, is a high priority.

Relief efforts will continue for people displaced by the conflict in Bosnia and other republics of the former Yugoslavia. We will act in concert with other nations and the UN against the illegal smuggling of Chinese into this country. In concert with the tools of diplomatic, economic and military power, our humanitarian and refugee policies can bear results, as was evident in Haiti. We provided temporary safe haven at Guantanamo Naval Base for those Haitians who feared for their safety and left by sea until we helped restore democracy.

·III·
INTEGRATED REGIONAL APPROACHES

The United States is a genuinely global power. Our policy toward each of the world's regions reflects our overall strategy tailored to their unique challenges and opportunities. This section highlights the application of our strategy to each of the world's regions; our broad objectives and thrust, rather than an exhaustive list of all our policies and interests. It illustrates how we integrate our commitment to the promotion of democracy and the enhancement of American prosperity with our security requirements to produce a mutually reinforcing policy.

Europe and Eurasia

Our strategy of enlargement and engagement is central to U.S. policy toward post–Cold War Europe. European stability is vital to our own security, a lesson we have learned twice at great cost this century. Vibrant European economies mean more jobs for Americans at home and investment opportunities abroad. With the collapse of the Soviet empire and the emergence of new democracies in its wake, the United States has an unparalleled opportunity to contribute toward a free and undivided Europe. Our goal is an integrated democratic Europe cooperating with the United States to keep the peace and promote prosperity.

The first and most important element of our strategy in Europe must be security through military strength and cooperation. The Cold War is over, but war itself is not over.

As we know, war continues in the former Yugoslavia. While that war does not pose a direct threat to our security or warrant unilateral U.S. involvement, U.S. policy is focused on five goals: achieving a political settlement in Bosnia that preserves the country's territorial integrity and provides a viable future for all its peoples; preventing the spread of the fighting into a broader Balkan war that could threaten both allies and the stability of new democratic states in Central and Eastern Europe; stemming the destabilizing flow of refugees from the conflict; halting the slaughter of innocents; and helping to support NATO's central role in post–Cold War Europe while maintaining our role in shaping Europe's security architecture.

Our leadership paved the way to NATO's February 1994 ultimatum that ended the heavy Serb bombardment of Sarajevo, Bosnia's capital. Our diplomatic leadership brought an end to the fighting between the Muslims and Croats in Bosnia and helped establish a bicommunal Bosnian-Croat Federation. Since April 1994, we have been working with the warring parties through the Contact Group (United States, Russia, United Kingdom, France and Germany) to help the parties reach a negotiated settlement. Our goal is to bring an end to the war in Bosnia consistent with the Contact Group plan which would preserve Bosnia as a single state within its existing borders while providing for an equitable division of territory between the Muslim-Croat Federation and the Bosnian-Serb entity. While we have not yet succeeded in achieving a political settlement, diplomatic efforts in the final months of 1994 helped produce a cease-fire and a cessation of hostilities agreement that took effect on January 1, 1995. On this basis, efforts are now underway with our Contact Group partners to renew negotiations on a political settlement based on the Contact Group plan.

Should these new diplomatic efforts falter, we remain prepared to move forward with our proposal at the UN to lift the arms embargo on Bosnia-Herzegovina, multilaterally. We remain strongly opposed to a unilateral lifting of the arms embargo as a step that would have grave consequences for NATO and U.S. interests. Should large-scale fighting resume and UN troops need to be withdrawn, the President has agreed, in principle, to provide U.S. support, including the use of ground forces, to a NATO-led operation to help assure a safe withdrawal. We also remain prepared to help implement a final peace settlement in Bosnia.

As we work to resolve that tragedy and ease the suffering of its victims we also need to transform European and trans-Atlantic institutions so they can better address such conflicts and advance Europe's integration. Many institutions will play a role, including the European Union (EU), the Western European Union (WEU), the Council of

Europe (CE), the Organization for Security and Cooperation in Europe (OSCE) and the United Nations. But NATO, history's greatest political-military alliance, must be central to that process.

The NATO alliance will remain the anchor of American engagement in Europe and the linchpin of trans-Atlantic security. That is why we must keep it strong, vital and relevant. For the United States and its allies, NATO has always been far more than a transitory response to a temporary threat. It has been a guarantor of European democracy and a force for European stability. That is why its mission endures even though the Cold War has receded into the past. And that is why its benefits are so clear to Europe's new democracies.

Only NATO has the military forces, the integrated command structure, the broad legitimacy and the habits of cooperation that are essential to draw in new participants and respond to new challenges. One of the deepest transformations within the trans-Atlantic community over the past half-century occurred because the armed forces of our respective nations trained, studied and marched through their careers together. It is not only the compatibility of our weapons, but the camaraderie of our warriors that provide the sinews behind our mutual security guarantees and our best hope for peace.

Since the end of the Cold War, the United States has significantly reduced the level of U.S. military forces stationed in Europe. We have determined that a force of roughly 100,000 U.S. military personnel assigned to U.S. European command will preserve U.S. influence and leadership in NATO and provide a deterrent posture that is visible to all Europeans. While we continue to examine the proper mix of forces, this level of permanent presence, augmented by forward deployed naval forces and reinforcements available from the United States, is sufficient to respond to plausible crises and contributes to stability in the region. Such a force level also provides a sound basis for U.S. participation in multinational training and preserves the capability to deter or respond to larger threats in Europe and to support limited NATO operations "out of area."

With the end of the Cold War, NATO's mission is evolving; today NATO plays a crucial role helping to manage ethnic and national conflict in Europe. With U.S. leadership, NATO has provided the muscle behind efforts to bring about a peaceful settlement in the former Yugoslavia. NATO air power enforces the UN-mandated no-fly zone and provides support to UN peacekeepers. NATO stands ready to help support the peace once the parties reach an agreement.

With the adoption of the U.S. initiative, Partnership for Peace, at the January 1994 summit, NATO is playing an increasingly important role in our strategy of European integration, extending the scope of our security cooperation to the new democracies of Europe. Twenty-five nations, including Russia, have already joined the partnership, which will pave the way for a growing program of military cooperation and political consultation. Partner countries are sending representatives to NATO headquarters near Brussels and to a military coordination cell at Mons—the site of Supreme Headquarters Allied Powers Europe (SHAPE). Joint exercises have taken place in Poland and the Netherlands. In keeping with our strategy of enlargement, PFP is open to all former members of the Warsaw Pact as well as other European states. Each partner will set the scope and pace of its cooperation with NATO.

The North Atlantic Treaty has always looked to the addition of members who shared the Alliance's purposes and its values, its commitment to respect borders and international law, and who could add to its strength; indeed, NATO has expanded three times since its creation. In January 1994, President Clinton made it plain that "the question is no longer whether NATO will take on new members, but when and how we will do so." Last December, we and our Allies began a steady, deliberate and transparent process that will lead to NATO expansion.

During 1995, we will come to agreement with our allies on the process and principles, and we will share our conclusions with the members of the Partnership for Peace (PFP). Once this effort is complete, NATO can turn to the question of candidates and timing. Each nation will be considered individually. No non-member of NATO will have a veto.

Expanding the Alliance will promote our interests by reducing the risk of instability or conflict in Europe's eastern half—the region where two world wars and the Cold War began. It will help assure that no part of Europe will revert to a zone of great power competition or a sphere of influence. It will build confidence, and give new democracies a powerful incentive to consolidate their reforms. And each potential member will be judged according to the strength of its democratic institutions and its capacity to contribute to the goals of the Alliance.

As the President has made clear, NATO expansion will not be aimed at replacing one division of Europe with a new one, but to enhance the security of all European states, members and non-members alike. In this regard, we have a major stake in ensuring that Russia is engaged as a vital participant in European security affairs. We are committed to a growing, healthy NATO-Russia relationship and want to see Russia closely involved in the

Partnership for Peace. Recognizing that no single institution can meet every challenge to peace and stability in Europe, we have begun a process that will strengthen the Organization for Security and Cooperation in Europe (OSCE) and enhance its conflict prevention and peacekeeping capabilities.

The second element of the new strategy for Europe is economic. The United States seeks to build on vibrant and open market economies, the engines that have given us the greatest prosperity in human history over the last several decades in Europe and in the United States. To this end, we strongly support the process of European integration embodied in the European Union and seek to deepen our partnership with the EU in support of our economic goals, but also commit ourselves to the encouragement of bilateral trade and investment in countries not part of the EU.

The nations of the European Union face particularly significant economic challenges with nearly 20 million people unemployed and, in Germany's case, the extraordinarily high costs of unification. Among the Atlantic nations, economic stagnation has clearly eroded public support in finances for outward-looking foreign policies and for greater integration. We are working closely with our West European partners to expand employment and promote long-term growth, building on the results of the Detroit Jobs Conference and the Naples G-7 Summit. A White House–sponsored Trade and Investment Conference for Central and Eastern Europe took place in Cleveland in January.

In Northern Ireland, the Administration is implementing a package of initiatives to promote the peace process. The Secretary of Commerce led a Trade and Investment mission to Belfast in December 1994, and in April the President will host a White House Conference in Philadelphia on Trade and Investment in Northern Ireland.

As we work to strengthen our own economies, we must know that we serve our own prosperity and our security by helping the new market reforms in the new democracies in Europe's East that will help to deflate the region's demagogues. It will help ease ethnic tensions. It will help new democracies take root.

In Russia, Ukraine and the other new independent states of the former Soviet Union, the economic transformation undertaken will go down as one of the great historical events of this century. The Russian Government has made remarkable progress toward privatizing the economy (over 50 percent of the Russian Gross Domestic Product is now generated by the private sector) and reducing inflation, and Ukraine has taken bold steps of its own to institute much-needed economic reforms. But much remains to be done to build on the reform momentum to assure durable economic recovery and social protection. President Clinton has given strong and consistent support to this unprecedented reform effort, and has mobilized the international community to provide structural economic assistance, for example, securing agreement by the G-7 to make available four billion dollars in grants and loans as Ukraine implemented economic reform.

The short-term difficulties of taking Central and Eastern Europe into Western economic institutions will be more than rewarded if they succeed and if they are customers for America's and Western Europe's goods and services tomorrow. That is why this Administration has been committed to increase support substantially for market reforms in the new states of the former Soviet Union, and why we have continued our support for economic transition in Central and Eastern Europe, while also paying attention to measures that can overcome the social dislocations which have resulted largely from the collapse of the Soviet-dominated regional trading system.

Ultimately, the success of market reforms to the East will depend more on trade than aid. No one nation has enough resources to markedly change the future of those countries as they move to free market systems. One of our priorities, therefore, is to reduce trade barriers with the former communist states.

The third and final imperative of this new strategy is to support the growth of democracy and individual freedoms that has begun in Russia, the nations of the former Soviet Union and Europe's former communist states. The success of these democratic reforms makes us all more secure; they are the best answer to the aggressive nationalism and ethnic hatreds unleashed by the end of the Cold War. Nowhere is democracy's success more important to us all than in these countries.

This will be the work of generations. There will be wrong turns and even reversals, as there have been in all countries throughout history. But as long as these states continue their progress toward democracy and respect the rights of their own and other people, that they understand the rights of their minorities and their neighbors, we will support their progress with a steady patience.

East Asia and the Pacific

East Asia is a region of growing importance for U.S. security and prosperity; nowhere are the strands of our three-pronged strategy more intertwined, nor is the need for continued U.S. engagement more evident. Now more than ever, security, open markets and democracy go hand in hand in our approach to this dynamic region. Last year, President Clinton laid out an integrated strategy—a New Pacific Community—which links security requirements with economic realities and our concern for democracy and human rights.

In thinking about Asia, we must remember that security is the first pillar of our new Pacific community. The United States is a Pacific nation. We have fought three wars there in this century. To deter regional aggression and secure our own interests, we will maintain an active presence and we will continue to lead. Our deep bilateral ties with allies such as Japan, South Korea, Australia, Thailand and the Philippines, and a continued American military presence will serve as the foundation for America's security role in the region. Currently, our forces number nearly 100,000 personnel in East Asia. In addition to performing the general forward deployment functions outlined above, they contribute to regional stability by deterring aggression and adventurism.

As a key element of our strategic commitment to the region, we are pursuing stronger efforts to combat the proliferation of weapons of mass destruction on the Korean Peninsula and in South Asia. In October 1994, we reached an important agreed framework with North Korea—stopping, and eventually eliminating, its nuclear weapons program—and an agreement with China, limiting its sales of ballistic missiles.

Another example of our security commitment to the Asia-Pacific region in this decade is our effort to develop multiple new arrangements to meet multiple threats and opportunities. We have supported new regional exchanges—such as the ASEAN Regional Forum—on the full range of common security challenges. These arrangements can enhance regional security and understanding through dialogue and transparency. These regional exchanges are grounded on the strong network of bilateral relationships that exist today.

The continuing tensions on the Korean Peninsula remain the principal threat to the peace and stability of the Asian region. We have worked assiduously with our South Korean and Japanese allies, with the People's Republic of China and with Russia, and with various UN organizations to resolve the problem of North Korea's nuclear program. We have also engaged in extensive negotiations with the Pyongyang government, and have worked out an agreed framework for replacing—over a ten-year period—North Korea's dangerous, plutonium-producing reactors with safer light water reactors. That effort will be accompanied by a willingness to improve bilateral political and economic ties with the North, commensurate with their continued cooperation to resolve the nuclear issue and to make progress on other issues of concern. Our long-run objective continues to be a non-nuclear, peacefully reunified Korean Peninsula. Our strong and active commitment to our South Korean allies and to the region is the foundation of this effort.

We are developing a broader engagement with the People's Republic of China that will encompass both our economic and strategic interests. That policy is best reflected in our decision to delink China's Most Favored Nation status from its record on human rights. We will also facilitate China's entry into international trade organizations, such as the General Agreement on Tariffs and Trade if it undertakes the necessary obligations. Given its growing economic potential and already sizable military force, it is essential that China not become a security threat to the region. To that end, we are strongly promoting China's participation in regional security mechanisms to reassure its neighbors and assuage its own security concerns. We have also broadened our bilateral security dialogue with the Chinese and we are seeking to gain further cooperation from China in controlling the proliferation of weapons of mass destruction. We are also in the early stages of a dialogue with China on environmental and health challenges.

The second pillar of our engagement in Asia is our commitment to continuing and enhancing the economic prosperity that has characterized the region. Opportunities for economic progress continue to abound in Asia, and underlie our strong commitment to multilateral economic cooperation, principally through APEC. Today, the 18 member states of APEC—comprising about one-third of the world's population—produce $14 trillion and export $1.7 trillion of goods annually, about one-half of the world's totals. U.S. exports to APEC economies reached $300 billion last year, supporting nearly 2.6 million American jobs. U.S. investments in the region totaled over $140 million—about one-third of total U.S. direct foreign investment. A prosperous and open Asia Pacific is key to the economic health of the United States. The first APEC leaders meeting, hosted by President Clinton, is vivid testimony to the possibilities of stimulating regional economic cooperation as we saw in the recent APEC leaders statement at the second leaders meeting that accepted the goal of free trade within the region by early in the 21st century.

We are also working with our major bilateral trade partners to improve trade relations. The U.S. and Japan successfully completed a preliminary accord in September to bring about the implementation of the 1993 Framework Agreement, designed to open Japan's markets more to competitive U.S. goods and reduce the U.S. trade deficit. Since we delinked China's Most Favored Nation trade status from specific human rights considerations in May, U.S.-China trade has grown significantly. We continue to work closely with Beijing to resolve remaining bilateral and multilateral trade problems, such as intellectual property rights and market access. Unless the issue of intellectual property rights is resolved, economic sanctions will be imposed.

The third pillar of our policy in building a new Pacific community is to support democratic reform in the region. The new democratic states of Asia will have our strong support as they move forward to consolidate and expand democratic reforms.

Some have argued that democracy is somehow unsuited for Asia or at least for some Asian nations—that human rights are relative and that they simply mask Western cultural imperialism. These arguments are wrong. It is not Western imperialism, but the aspirations of Asian peoples themselves that explain the growing number of democracies and the growing strength of democracy movements everywhere in Asia. We support those aspirations and those movements.

Each nation must find its own form of democracy, and we respect the variety of democratic institutions that have grown in Asia. But there is no cultural justification for torture or tyranny. Nor do we accept repression cloaked in moral relativism. Democracy and human rights are universal yearnings and universal norms, just as powerful in Asia as elsewhere. We will continue to press for respect for human rights in countries as diverse as China and Burma.

The Western Hemisphere

The Western hemisphere, too, is a fertile field for a strategy of engagement and enlargement. Sustained improvements in the security situation there, including the resolution of border tensions, control of insurgencies and containment of pressures for arms proliferation, will be an essential underpinning of political and economic progress in the hemisphere.

The unprecedented triumph of democracy and market economies throughout the region offers an unparalleled opportunity to secure the benefits of peace and stability, and to promote economic growth and trade. At the Summit of the Americas, which President Clinton hosted in December, the 34 democratic nations of the hemisphere committed themselves for the first time to the goal of free trade in the region. They also agreed to a detailed plan of cooperative action in such diverse fields as health, education, environmental protection and the strengthening of democratic institutions. To assure that proposals in this plan are implemented, they called for a series of follow-on ministerial meetings over the next year and requested the active participation of the Organization of American States and the Inter-American Development Bank. The Summit ushered in a new era of hemispheric cooperation that would not have been possible without U.S. leadership and commitment.

NAFTA, ratified in December 1994, has strengthened economic ties, with substantial increases in U.S. exports to both Mexico and Canada, creating new jobs and new opportunities for American workers and business. The United States, Mexico and Canada have begun discussions to add Chile to NAFTA.

We remain committed to extending democracy to all of the region's people still blocked from controlling their own destinies. Our overarching objective is to preserve and defend civilian elected governments and strengthen democratic practices respectful of human rights. Working with the international community, we succeeded in reversing the coup in Haiti and restoring the democratically elected president and government. Our challenge now is to help the Haitian people consolidate their hard-won democracy and rebuild their country. With the restoration of democracy in Haiti, Cuba is the only country in the hemisphere still ruled by a dictator. The Cuban Democracy Act remains the framework for our policy toward Cuba; our goal is the peaceful establishment of democratic governance for the people of Cuba.

We are working with our neighbors through various hemispheric organizations, including the OAS, to invigorate regional cooperation. Both bilaterally and regionally, we seek to eliminate the scourge of drug trafficking, which poses a serious threat to democracy and security. We also seek to strengthen norms for defense establishments that are supportive of democracy, respect for human rights, and civilian control in defense matters. Finally, protecting the region's precious environmental resources is an important priority.

The Middle East, Southwest and South Asia

The United States has enduring interests in the Middle East, especially pursuing a comprehensive breakthrough to Middle East peace, assuring the security of Israel and our Arab friends, and maintaining the free flow of oil at reasonable prices. Our strategy is harnessed to the unique characteristics of the region and our vital interests there, as we work to extend the range of peace and stability.

We have made solid progress in the past two years. The President's efforts helped bring about many historic firsts—the handshake of peace between Prime Minister Rabin and Chairman Arafat on the White House lawn has been followed by the Jordan-Israel peace treaty, progress on eliminating the Arab boycott of Israel, and the establishment of ties between Israel and an increasing number of its Arab neighbors. But our efforts have not stopped there; on other bilateral tracks and through regional dialogue we are working to foster a durable peace and a comprehensive settlement, while our support for economic development can bring hope to all the peoples of the region.

In Southwest Asia, the United States remains focused on deterring threats to regional stability, particularly from Iraq and Iran as long as those states pose a threat to U.S. interests, to other states in the region, and to their own citizens. We have in place a dual containment strategy aimed at these two states, and will maintain our long-standing presence which has been centered on naval vessels in and near the Persian Gulf and prepositioned combat equipment. Since Operation Desert Storm, temporary deployments of land-based aviation forces, ground forces and amphibious units have supplemented our posture in the Gulf region. Operation Vigilant Warrior demonstrated our ability to rapidly reinforce the region in time of crisis.

We have made clear to Iraq it must comply with all the relevant Security Council resolutions, and we remain committed to supporting oppressed minorities in Iraq through Operations Provide Comfort and Southern Watch. Our policy is directed not against the people of Iraq, but against the aggressive behavior of the government. The October 1994 deployment, Vigilant Warrior, demonstrated again the need and our ability to respond quickly to threats to our allies.

Our policy toward Iran is aimed at changing the behavior of the Iranian government in several key areas, including Iran's efforts to obtain weapons of mass destruction and missiles, its support for terrorism and groups that oppose the peace process, its attempts to undermine friendly governments in the region and its dismal human rights record. We remain willing to enter into an authoritative dialogue with Iran to discuss the differences between us.

A key objective of our policy in the Gulf is to reduce the chances that another aggressor will emerge who would threaten the independence of existing states. Therefore, we will continue to encourage members of the Gulf Cooperation Council to work closely on collective defense and security arrangements, help individual GCC states meet their appropriate defense requirements and maintain our bilateral defense agreements.

South Asia has experienced an important expansion of democracy and economic reform, and our strategy is designed to help the peoples of that region enjoy the fruits of democracy and greater stability through efforts aimed at resolving long-standing conflict and implementing confidence building measures. The United States has engaged India and Pakistan in seeking agreement on steps to cap, reduce and ultimately eliminate their weapons of mass destruction and ballistic missile capabilities. Regional stability and improved bilateral ties are also important for America's economic interest in a region that contains a quarter of the world's population and one of its most important emerging markets.

In both the Middle East and South Asia, the pressure of expanding populations on natural resources is enormous. Growing desertification in the Middle East has strained relations over arable land. Pollution of the coastal areas in the Eastern Mediterranean, the Red Sea and the Gulf of Aqaba has degraded fish catches and hindered development. Water shortages stemming from overuse, contaminated water aquifers and riparian disputes threaten regional relations. In South Asia, high population densities and rampant pollution have exacted a tremendous toll on forests, biodiversity and the local environment.

Africa

Africa poses one of our greatest challenges and opportunities to enlarge the community of market democracies. Throughout Africa, U.S. policy supports democracy, sustainable economic development and resolution of conflicts through negotiation, diplomacy and peacekeeping. New policies will strengthen civil societies and mechanisms for conflict resolution, particularly where ethnic, religious and political tensions are acute. In particular, we will seek to identify and address the root causes of conflicts and disasters before they erupt.

The nexus of economic, political, social, ethnic and environmental challenges facing Africa can lead to a sense of "Afro-pessimism." However, if we can simultaneously address these challenges, we create a synergy that can stimulate development, resurrect societies and build hope. We encourage democratic reform in nations like Nigeria and Zaire to allow the people of these countries to enjoy responsive government. In Mozambique and Angola, we have played a leading role in bringing an end to two decades of civil war and promoting national reconciliation. For the first time, there is the prospect that all of southern Africa could enjoy the fruits of peace and prosperity. Throughout the continent—in Rwanda, Burundi, Liberia, Sudan and elsewhere—we work with the UN and regional organizations to encourage peaceful resolution of internal disputes.

Last year, South Africa held its first non-racial elections and created a Government of National Unity. We remain committed to addressing the socio-economic legacies of apartheid to ensure that democracy fully takes root in South Africa. During the state visit of Nelson Mandela, we announced formation of a bilateral commission to foster new cooperation between our nations. We must support the revolution of democracy sweeping the continent—on center stage in South Africa, and in quieter but no less dramatic ways in countries like Malawi, Benin, Niger and Mali. We need to encourage the creation of cultures of tolerance, flowering of civil society and the protection of human rights and human dignity.

Our humanitarian interventions, along with the international community, will address the grave circumstances in several nations on the continent. USAID's new "Greater Horn of Africa" initiative got ahead of the curve on a potential famine that threatened 25 million people, and moved beyond relief to support reconstruction and sustainable development. In Somalia, our forces broke through the chaos that prevented the introduction of relief supplies. U.S. forces prevented the death of hundreds of thousands of Somalis and then turned over the mission to UN peacekeepers from over a score of nations. In Rwanda, Sudan, Angola and Liberia, we have taken an active role in providing humanitarian relief to those displaced by violence.

Such efforts by the U.S. and the international community must be limited in duration and designed to give the peoples of a nation the opportunity to put their own house in order. In the final

Engagement and Enlargement: 1995–1996 139

analysis, the responsibility for the fate of a nation rests with its own people.

We are also working with regional organizations, non-governmental organizations and governments throughout Africa to address the urgent issues of population growth, spreading disease (including AIDS), environmental decline, enhancing the role of women in development, eliminating support for terrorism, demobilization of bloated militaries, relieving burdensome debt and expanding trade and investment ties to the countries of Africa.

Central to all these efforts will be strengthening the American constituency for Africa, drawing on the knowledge, experience and commitment of millions of Americans to enhance our nation's support for positive change in Africa. For example, the White House Conference on Africa, the first such gathering of regional experts ever sponsored by the White House, drew together more than 200 Americans from the Administration, Congress, business, labor, academia, religious groups, relief and development agencies, human rights groups and others to discuss Africa's future and the role that the United States can play in it. The President, Vice President, Secretary of State and National Security Advisor all participated in the conference, which produced a wealth of new ideas and new commitment to Africa.

·IV·
CONCLUSIONS

The clear and present dangers of the Cold War made the need for national security commitments and expenditures obvious to the American people. Today the task of mobilizing public support for national security priorities has become more complicated. The complex array of new dangers, opportunities and responsibilities outlined in this strategy come at a moment in our history when Americans are preoccupied with domestic concerns and when budgetary constraints are tighter than at any point in the last half century. Yet, in a more integrated and interdependent world, we simply cannot be successful in advancing our interests—political, military and economic—without active engagement in world affairs.

While Cold War threats have diminished, our nation can never again isolate itself from global developments. Domestic renewal will not succeed if we fail to engage abroad in open foreign markets, to promote democracy in key countries and to counter and contain emerging threats.

We are committed to enhancing U.S. national security in the most efficient and effective ways possible. We recognize that maintaining peace and ensuring our national security in a volatile world are expensive. The cost of any other course of action, however, would be immeasurably higher.

Our engagement abroad requires the active, sustained bipartisan support of the American people and the U.S. Congress. Of all the elements contained in this strategy, none is more important than this: our Administration is committed to explaining our security interests and objectives to the nation; to seeking the broadest possible public and congressional support for our security programs and investments; and to exerting our leadership in the world in a manner that reflects our best national values and protects the security of this great and good nation.